Winter

Recipes Inspired by Nature's Bounty

Time-Life Books is a division of Time Life Inc.
Time-Life is a trademark of Time Warner Inc. U.S.A.

TIME-LIFE CUSTOM PUBLISHING
Vice President and Publisher: Terry Newell
Associate Publisher: Teresa Hartnett
Managing Editor: Donia Ann Steele
Director of New Product Development: Quentin McAndrew
Director of Sales: Neil Levin
Director of Financial Operations: J. Brian Birky

WILLIAMS-SONOMA
Founder/Vice-Chairman: Chuck Williams
Book Buyer: Victoria Kalish

Produced by
WELDON OWEN INC.
President: John Owen
Vice President and Publisher: Wendely Harvey
Chief Financial Officer: Larry Partington
Associate Publisher: Lisa Chaney Atwood
Consulting Editor: Norman Kolpas
Copy Editor: Sharon Silva
Production Director: Stephanie Sherman
Production Manager: Jen Dalton
Production Editor: Katherine Withers Cobbs
Design: Angela Williams
Food Photographer: Penina
Food and Prop Stylist: Pouké
Assistant Food Photographer: Martin Dunham
Assistant Food Stylist: Michelle Syracuse
Illustrations: Thorina Rose
Co-Editions Director: Derek Barton
Director of International Sales: Stuart Laurence

Manufactured by Toppan Printing Co., (H.K.) Ltd.
Printed in China

First Printing 1997
10 9 8 7 6 5 4 3 2 1

Library of Congress
Cataloging-in-Publication Data:

Weir, Joanne
    Winter : recipes inspired by nature's bounty / Joanne Weir.
        p. cm. -- (Williams-Sonoma seasonal celebration)
    Includes index.
    ISBN 0-7835-4609-2
    1. Cookery.   2. Winter.   I. Title.   II. Series.
TX714.W3343   1997
641.5'64--DC20   96-34195
                                                          CIP

A Note on Weights and Measures:
All recipes include customary U.S. and metric measurements.
Metric conversions are based on a standard developed for these
books and have been rounded off. Actual weights may vary.

Winter

Recipes Inspired by Nature's Bounty

Joanne Weir

Winter

Brussels sprouts thrive in mild climates throughout the damp winter season.

The pale inner leaves from a head of escarole are less bitter and more tender than the outer ones.

While winter's cool earth harbors its energy in anticipation of spring's bounty, the coldest season nonetheless produces a generous harvest of its own. Robust greens such as kale and escarole (Batavian endive), along with bitter members of the chicory family, thrive in the waning sunlight. Roots and tubers such as parsnips, potatoes and Jerusalem artichokes grow plump and sweet in the cold ground. In milder climes, citrus crops flourish, bringing a burst of bright color and zesty flavor to even the grayest days.

Gathered together in the warmth of the kitchen, winter's ingredients are transformed into comforting dishes that build upon their hearty nature. Root vegetables simmer in soup kettles or add rich flavors and textures to stews and pot pies. Sturdy winter greens, sautéed in butter with garlic and herbs, become the perfect complement to the season's crisp, golden brown roasts of chicken, goose and pork. Autumn's pantry staples, in the form of hard-shelled winter squashes and some hardy tree fruits, also figure in the season's classic recipes.

Selecting Winter Ingredients

Winter Vegetables. The best winter vegetables are generally those that thrive under adverse climate conditions. When selecting hard-shelled **squashes,** choose specimens that feel heavy for their size and have good color; avoid cracked squashes, which can spoil quickly, or those with soft spots that indicate decay. If you buy precut portions of a large squash, wrap tightly in plastic wrap, refrigerate and use within 3 days.

Winter's robust greens, including **watercress, frisée, kale, escarole** (Batavian endive) and **Belgian endive** (chicory/witloof), taste best when harvested young and tender. In particular, conical heads of Belgian endive should be small, compact and pale. **Brussels sprouts** should have solid, tightly packed heads that look crisp and fresh.

The earth shelters many winter vegetables from the season's extremes. **Bulb fennel** and **leeks** should have crisp, white bulb ends and healthy-looking leaves with no signs of wilting. **Parsnips** should feel firm and heavy and be blemish free; smaller ones have finer flavor and texture. When choosing **potatoes, sweet potatoes, yams** and **Jerusalem artichokes,** look for skins in good condition, fairly free of eyes and, in the case of potatoes, any green spots.

The scent of **fresh herbs** brings a touch of warmth to the winter kitchen. Choose herbs with brightly hued leaves free of discoloration or wilting. You might even grow herbs yourself from seed or from plants bought at a nursery. All the herbs shown on page 10 can be grown throughout the winter months on sunny windowsills or, in milder climates, in outdoor gardens.

Mushrooms in good condition are firm and plump and feel slightly spongy, with skins neither too dry nor overly moist. They should also have a clean earthen scent. Do not buy more than you will use in a few days.

Dried beans may be bought in bulk and stored for many months at room temperature in airtight containers. Those that have not been kept for too long, however, cook more quickly and have a finer texture and flavor. Purchase the beans from a shop with a high turnover of stock and look for those with bright, shiny skins free of wrinkles or other indications of improper handling.

The tangelo, also called Minneola, is a hybrid of the tangerine and the pomelo or grapefruit.

Winter Fruits. Many of the season's fruits are hardy autumn crops that endure cold storage. Crisp, juicy **apples** should feel firm to the touch, particularly larger specimens that mature more quickly. **Pears,** generally sold underripe and firm, will ripen at room temperature. The same quality guidelines apply to **quinces,** which are green when unripe and ripen at room temperature to a pale yellow and a sweet scent. The best **citrus fruits** have shiny, lustrous skins with no traces of mold; they should feel heavy for their size, indicating juiciness. In general, citrus skins with large pores indicate a thick peel; smooth skins with small pores denote a thinner peel.

When choosing **pomegranates,** seek out larger ones with shiny skins for the most and the juiciest kernels. **Persimmons** should have smooth skins, bright color and intact green caps. The Hachiya persimmon is soft when ripe and should be eaten immediately; hard ones will soften at room temperature in about a week. The Fuyu variety is eaten while still crisp like an apple.

The brown, fuzzy skins of **kiwifruits** offer few clues to quality, although they should be free of cuts or bruises. Press the fruit gently with your fingertips; it gives slightly when ripe. Hard ones will ripen at room temperature. **Cranberries** should feel firm when lightly squeezed and have shiny, bright red skins; discard any that are wrinkled or discolored. The berries may be refrigerated for up to 3 weeks or frozen for up to 3 months.

Even winter's **dried fruits** have varying degrees of freshness. Look for specimens that are plump and have good color, signs that they have been recently dried. They will be moister and more flavorful.

Crisp, green turnip tops are delicious cooked like kale as a robust winter green.

Winter Vegetables

Winter Greens

1. Bulb Fennel
Available year-round, this bulbous cluster of stalk bases has a crisp texture resembling celery and a mild anise flavor. It may be eaten raw in salads or cooked on its own or with other ingredients, like fish or chicken, that are complemented by its sweetness.

2. Watercress
Available year-round, this spicy-sweet, tender member of the mustard family may be enjoyed raw in salads, where it is particularly prized for its sharp, peppery taste; cooked with eggs, poultry or seafood; or puréed in a sauce or in soups.

3. Frisée
These thin, frilly leaves, which grow in loosely bunched heads, are most often eaten raw in salads. Like their cousins escarole (Batavian endive) and dandelions, they have an appealing bitterness that is at its mildest in the paler inner leaves.

4. Kale
At its peak of season throughout the cold months, this hardy member of the mustard family is cooked and enjoyed for its strong, spicy flavor. The leaves of this loose, long-leaved green come in different shapes and in colors ranging from blue-green and red (pictured near right) to purple, yellow or white. Many varieties are sold, but the leaves generally have serrated edges and a crinkly surface, leading the most commonly available type also to be known as curly kale (pictured far right).

5. Escarole
Variety of chicory distinguished by its broad, bright green leaves, which grow in loose heads. Escarole has a refreshingly bitter edge, while being notably less bitter than other relatives of the chicory family. Generally eaten raw in salads. Also known as Batavian endive.

6. Leeks
Available throughout winter, these long, cylindrical members of the onion family have white root ends, dark green leaves and a delicate, sweet flavor that has earned them the

French nickname of "poor man's asparagus." The white parts are more tender and have a finer flavor, although the greens are often included in long-simmering dishes. Because leeks are grown in sandy soil, they require thorough washing with cold running water to remove any grit lodged between their multilayered leaves.

7. Belgian Endives
Packed in distinctive cone-shaped heads, these crisp, white, spear-shaped leaves may be edged in pale yellow-green or pinkish red. They have a light, refreshing bitterness that is mildest in smaller heads and comes through whether enjoyed raw or cooked. Also known as chicory or witloof.

8. Brussels Sprouts
This species of cabbage was first selectively bred in Belgium in the 13th century to form the familiar small, bite-sized balls, which grow in rows on a heavy stalk. They are widely available from autumn almost to the end of winter. Brussels sprouts may sometimes be found in farmers' markets still attached to their stalk,

generally pale gold. Some aficionados claim they give off a faint scent reminiscent of apricots. Their fine flavor and tender texture are best appreciated when only lightly cooked. Picked wild in woodlands, particularly where oak and beech trees grow, they are now also cultivated in the Pacific Northwest. Rare black chanterelles are also sometimes found.

12. Porcini

Meaning "little pigs" in Italian, these plump mushrooms have brown caps and thick stems with a tender texture and a rich, earthy taste that hints of hazelnut. Found in the wild throughout North America, they are also known by the French *cèpes,* by the Latin *Boletus edulis,* and in Britain by the descriptive "penny buns." The mushrooms taste best when grilled, sautéed or baked, although they may also be thinly sliced and eaten raw.

13. Shiitake Mushrooms

Originally from Asia but now widely cultivated in the United States and Europe, these rich mushrooms have a meaty taste and texture and are often cooked in dishes featuring red meat. The broad, fairly flat circular caps are dark, velvety brown. The stems are tough and must be trimmed away before cooking.

Chili Peppers

14. Jalapeño Chilies

Among the dozens of commercially cultivated chilies, these moderately hot peppers are arguably the most common. Jalapeños generally measure 2–3 inches (5–7.5 cm) in length and about 1 inch (2.5 cm) wide. They are usually sold in their immature dark green state, although ripened red ones may also be found. When handling any hot chili peppers, take great care to avoid touching your eyes or any other sensitive areas because the chilies—particularly their seeds and pale interior membranes, or "veins"—contain volatile oils that can cause painful burning. Wash your hands well with warm, soapy water after handling chilies.

15. Serrano Chilies

These small, slender chilies are noticeably hotter than jalapeños and may be found in both their underripe green and ripened red forms. See the cautionary note in the previous entry regarding working with hot chilies.

although they are more commonly sold already separated from it.

Mushrooms

9. Button Mushrooms

Harvested soon after they emerge from the soil, when their caps are still small and tightly closed with almost no stem visible, these immature cultivated mushrooms are sometimes said to resemble buttons. They have a fine texture and mild flavor and are excellent eaten raw in salads or lightly and quickly cooked.

10. Hedgehog Mushrooms

Fancifully thought to resemble hedgehogs, these wild woodland mushrooms are distinguished by their orange caps, white stems and compact shapes. Eaten cooked, often in egg or rice dishes, they are enjoyed for their fine, slightly tangy flavor, pale color and succulent texture. Known in French as *pied de mouton,* "sheep's foot."

11. Chanterelles

These trumpet-shaped mushrooms, which average 2–3 inches (5–7.5 cm) in length, are

Winter Herbs, Vegetables and Pantry

Winter Squashes

1. Hubbard Squash
Although it has an unattractive, murky yellow or greenish gray shell, this large, irregularly shaped squash contains flavorful, rich orange flesh.

2. Acorn Squash
The name derives from the acornlike shape of this medium-sized squash, which measures up to 8 inches (20 cm) in length and has a ribbed, dark green shell that turns orange with storage. The orange flesh has a mild, sweet flavor and light, smooth texture best complemented by baking.

3. Butternut Squash
Cylindrical squash up to 12 inches (30 cm) long, its flower end slightly enlarged to a bulb-like shape. Butternut squashes have bright orange, moist, fairly sweet flesh.

4. Turban Squash
This winter squash variety is distinguished by the small, turban-shaped top—orange with blue-green stripes—that crowns a flattened, circular, bumpy orange base up to 15 inches (37.5 cm) in diameter. Its rich flesh is bright orange.

Herbs

5. Mint
Refreshing herb used to flavor a variety of dishes from light meats to vegetables to desserts. Spearmint is the variety most commonly used in cooking.

6. Chives
These long, thin, green shoots contribute a mild flavor reminiscent of the onion, to which they are related.

7. Sage
Fragrant herb used either fresh or dried in European and Middle Eastern cuisines. Complements fresh or cured pork, lamb, veal or poultry, and some sauces and salads.

8. Thyme
Eastern Mediterranean herb with fragrant, clean-tasting small leaves that marry well with poultry, light meats, seafood or vegetables.

9. Parsley
Widely popular fresh herb native to southern Europe. Available in two main types: the more common curly-leaf parsley, traditionally used as a garnish; and flat-leaf parsley, also known as Italian parsley, with a more pronounced flavor that makes it preferable as a seasoning.

10. Rosemary
Mediterranean herb with needlelike leaves, sometimes decked in tiny blue flowers. Highly aromatic, rosemary goes well with lamb, veal, pork, poultry, seafood and vegetables.

11. Bay Leaves
Pungent, spicy dried whole leaves of the bay laurel tree, used to season simmered dishes, including soups, braises and stews; in mari-

nades; and in pickling mixtures. French bay leaves, sometimes found in specialty-food shops, are milder and sweeter than the bay leaves commonly grown in the United States.

Roots and Tubers

12. Rutabagas
These spherical, ivory-and-purple-skinned members of the cabbage family resemble large turnips. They have sweet, pale yellow-orange flesh and a firm texture. Also known as swedes or Swedish turnips.

13. Jerusalem Artichokes
Although many people consider the taste of these tubers to resemble that of artichokes, they are not related. Jerusalem is most likely a corruption of the Italian *girasole,* for the sunflowers

tasting flesh that, depending upon the variety, may range from ivory-white to pale red. Generally good for boiling.

18. Baking Potatoes

Distinguished by their large, elongated size and shape and their thick, brown skins, these potatoes have dry, mealy textures that make them the perfect choice for baking, mashing or deep-frying. Also known as russet or Idaho potatoes.

19. Baby Turnips

Immature specimens of the turnip, a root vegetable of the cabbage family, which begin to appear in late winter and are prized for their sweetness and tenderness.

20. Parsnips

These ivory roots, similar in shape and texture to carrots, are never eaten raw. When cooked, they have a sweet, rich, almost nutlike taste. Wintertime cold helps develop parsnips' sweet flavor by transforming their starch into sugar.

21. Beets

The earliest beets find their way into markets in late winter. Most common are red beets, although golden, pink, white, and even red-and-white varieties may be found.

Dried Beans

22. Great Northern Beans

Common variety of white, kidney-shaped bean smaller than Italian cannellini and larger than navy beans. Great Northerns may be substituted for either variety.

23. Black Beans

Robust, somewhat mealy beans distinguished by their relatively small size and black skins. Also called turtle beans.

24. Navy Beans

Small, white, thin-skinned oval beans, similar to cannellini or Great Northerns. Also known as soldier or Boston beans.

25. Red Beans

Resembling small, dark kidney beans, with a similar texture but a slightly sweeter taste.

26. Cannellini

Popular Italian variety of small, white, thin-skinned oval beans, similar to Great Northern or navy beans.

27. Flageolets

Small, pale green beans harvested and dried before they mature. A specialty of Brittany in northern France, they are now also being grown in the United States.

to which the plant is related. The small, knobby tubers have brown or purplish red skins that are most easily removed after cooking. They can also be eaten raw, unpeeled, in salads.

14. Celery Root

Also known as celeriac or celery knob. This hardy winter vegetable, a large, knobby root related to the plant that gives us the more familiar celery stalks, has a sweet, rich flavor reminiscent of its cousin. Celery root may be cooked, or shredded and eaten raw in salads.

15. Yams

Not the true, starchy yams of Africa, these are in fact a variety of sweet potato native to the Caribbean, with dark skins and deep orange flesh that becomes sweet when cooked.

16. Sweet Potatoes

Although these tubers resemble potatoes in form, they come from a tropical American cousin of the morning glory and have light tan to deep red skins and pale yellow to orange flesh prized for its sweetness. The light-skinned variety is the most common. Sweet potatoes may be cooked in any of the ways used for regular potatoes; baking, however, intensifies their natural sweetness, so they are cooked in the oven rather than boiled when intended for mashing.

17. Red Potatoes

Red-skinned potatoes of various types, ranging in size from small to medium, with creamy-

Winter Fruits

Apples

1. Granny Smith
Native to Australia, these apples have bright green skins and crisp, juicy flesh with a refreshing tartness. Most often eaten raw, they also hold their shape well when cooked.

2. McIntosh
These slightly tart, juicy, tender apples, which originated in Canada, have distinctive red-and-green skins. Excellent for eating, baking and making applesauce.

3. Pippin
Fruits with firm, green to yellow-green skin and dense, slightly tart, refreshing flesh. Delicious raw or cooked.

Citrus Fruits

4. Yellow Grapefruits
At their peak in winter, the large citrus fruits—named for the grapelike bunches they form on the tree—are enjoyed for their bracingly tart-sweet flavor. Also called white grapefruits, the yellow variety have pale yellow skins and whitish yellow flesh.

5. Ruby Grapefruits
Often sweeter than yellow grapefruits, pink- or red-fleshed varieties have an orange-red blush on their skins and dark, sweet flesh. The Ruby variety from Texas is among the sweetest.

6. Blood Oranges
Available throughout the winter, these sweet, aromatic, small- to medium-sized oranges are distinguished by the reddish blush on their skin and their sweet, intensely flavorful, deep red flesh and juice.

7. Kumquats
Resembling elongated, miniature oranges, these tiny fruits are usually eaten whole; the sweetness of their skins balances the tartness of their flesh.

8. Pomelos
Generally thought to be ancestors of the grapefruit, these largest citrus fruits have thick, bumpy skins and bittersweet, seedless flesh that ranges from yellow to pink to red. Also sometimes spelled pummelo.

9. Mandarins and Tangerines
Two interchangeable terms for a wide variety of small- to medium-sized fruits with loose peels and mild, sweet flesh. At their peak in mid- to late December, they are a traditional holiday favorite. Among the more familiar types are sweet, seedless Satsumas, originally from Japan; Clementines, a flavorful, seedless North African cross between a mandarin and a Seville orange; and the Dancy, an aromatic American hybrid.

10. Lemons
One of the most familiar citrus varieties, these year-round fruits have bright yellow skins, pale yellow flesh and a sharply acidic juice that sparks both savory and sweet dishes.

11. Tangelos
A cross between a tangerine and a pomelo or grapefruit, these sweet-tart fruits resemble large oranges with knobs at their stem ends. Also known by the name Minneola.

12. Navel Oranges
Available from early to midwinter, this orange variety gets its name from the indentation in the skin at its flower end. These large oranges have sweet, juicy flesh, are easily peeled and are virtually seedless.

Other Tree Fruits

13. Quinces
Middle Eastern in origin and grown today primarily in the Mediterranean and South America, these ancient fruits resemble in shape large, slightly lumpy apples or pears. Unpleasantly hard and rough-textured when raw, the flesh softens when cooked and turns a lovely pink. High in pectin, quinces are frequently made

16. Persimmons
Native to Asia, persimmons are enjoyed for their bright orange color, their lustrous smooth skins and the delectable sweetness of their jellylike orange flesh. Heart-shaped Hachiya persimmons, shown here, are the most widely available. They must be ripened to a point of mushy softness, or they will taste unpleasantly astringent. Fuyu persimmons, a more rounded variety, can be enjoyed while still as crisp as an apple, although they eventually soften.

17. Bosc Pears
Medium-to-large, tapered pears with russeted yellow skins and firm, slightly grainy flesh with a buttery, spicy taste. Picked or purchased when unripe and still very hard, Bosc pears will ripen and soften slightly when left at room temperature. Good for eating raw or for cooking.

Berries

18. Cranberries
Round, tart berries, grown primarily in wet, sandy coastal lands—or bogs—in the northeastern United States. Available fresh from late autumn to the end of December and frozen year-round, these deep red berries feature on many holiday tables.

Dried Fruits

19. Prunes
Dried plums, prunes are prized for their rich flavor and dense, fairly moist flesh.

20. Golden Raisins
These dried, sweet seedless grapes are also known as sultanas.

21. Dried Figs
The two most common forms of dried figs are those made from the Black Mission variety, which has a dark, dense flesh and an intense flavor; and the golden Calimyrna variety, prized for its sweet, nutty taste.

22. Dried Cherries
Kiln-dried cherries are generally made from pitted sour red cherries, with a little sugar added as a preservative.

23. Dried Apricots
Pitted whole or halved apricots develop a sweet, slightly tangy taste and a slightly chewy texture when dried.

24. Dried Cranberries
Cranberries (see above) are generally lightly sugared and then kiln-dried, which intensifies their flavor and deep red color, while giving them a shape and texture similar to raisins.

into jams or jellies. Like apples or pears, they should be skinned and cored before cooking, and their flesh must be rubbed with lemon juice to prevent discoloration.

14. Pomegranates
The name pomegranate is derived from the French for "apples with seeds." Sometimes called Chinese apples, these large, spherical, heavy fruits have leathery skins that range from yellow-orange to red to deep purple. Inside, an abundance of tightly packed kernels, each encased in ruby-red flesh, is embedded in spongy white membranes. The kernels may be eaten on their own, their tart-sweet pulp sucked away, or used as an edible garnish. More often, however, pomegranate juice is extracted as a flavoring, sometimes sweetened and boiled down to make a syrup. Commercial grenadine syrup is made from pomegranate juice.

15. Kiwifruits
Kiwis, as they are sometimes called, have fuzzy brown skins that conceal a bright green, soft, juicy, sweet flesh with a flavor reminiscent of melon and berries. When ripe, they yield gently to the touch; firm ones ripen under refrigeration in several days. Asian in origin, they are also known as Chinese gooseberries.

Winter Techniques

SOME OF WINTER'S FAVORED COOKING TECHNIQUES are undertaken with both aesthetic and practical goals in mind. Hazelnuts, for example, are toasted to remove their skins for the sake of appearance and to impart a more robust taste and texture. By the same token, poultry roasts are trussed for the oven so they look more attractive and cook more evenly. When the bird is done, its pan juices are deglazed and thickened into a rich gravy—a mainstay of cold-weather menus.

Other seasonal techniques yield up bright flavors that seem to chase away winter's chill, whether in the form of just-shucked oysters with their bracing taste of the sea, freshly cracked crab or plump segments of sunshine-colored citrus fruits.

Segmenting Citrus Fruits

Recipes in which citrus fruits—here, Ruby grapefruit—are featured often call for segments, or sections, to be cut away from the pith and membranes.

Using a sharp knife, cut a thick slice off the top and the bottom of each fruit, exposing the pulp. Hold the fruit upright and slice off the peel in thick strips, cutting around the contours of the fruit.

Hold the peeled fruit over a bowl. Using the knife, carefully cut between the fruit and membrane on either side of each segment to free it, letting it drop into the bowl with the juices. Discard any seeds.

Toasting Hazelnuts

Toasting nuts enriches their flavor and gives them a crunchier texture. In the case of hazelnuts (filberts), it also loosens their skins for removal. Roast all nuts in an oven preheated to 350°F (180°C).

Spread the nuts in a baking pan and toast until fragrant and lightly browned, 5–7 minutes. Let cool. Place the nuts between 2 layers of a kitchen towel and then rub them with the towel to loosen the skins.

Cleaning Whole Crab

Whether you cook a whole crab yourself or buy it already cooked from a seafood shop, these steps will help you extract all the meat. The job gets easier with practice.

Twist off the legs and claws. Pry off the small, triangular shell flap (left) from the underside of the crab. Insert your thumbs in the crevice between the top shell and the body and pull them apart.

Remove and discard the feather-shaped gills (left) and any gray intestines, rinsing well. Cut the body in half. Use a lobster cracker to crack open the legs and claws. Remove all the meat.

Shucking Oysters

Buy fresh oysters alive, in the shell, from a good seafood merchant. To open an oyster shell, hold it in a kitchen towel, flat side up and hinge toward you. Pry open using a short, sturdy oyster knife as demonstrated below.

Push the knife into one side of the oyster's hinge and twist to open. Run the blade completely around the oyster to sever the muscle holding the shells together, then lift off the top shell.

Trussing Poultry

A turkey is trussed before roasting to give it a compact shape that cooks more evenly and looks more attractive. Diligent basting during roasting yields moist results.

Stuff the turkey. Tie the drumsticks together with kitchen string. Place the turkey, breast side up, on a rack in a roasting pan. Secure the wings against the bird by tucking their tips beneath the breast (left).

Making Gravy

Gravy can be made in many different ways, but most involve deglazing congealed juices from the roasting pan and adding body with a thickening agent—here, cornstarch (cornflour)—then boiling until the gravy thickens.

Remove the roast from the pan and pour off the fat. Place the pan over high heat. Pour in a liquid—here, chicken stock—and deglaze the pan, stirring to remove any browned bits from the bottom.

Boil the liquid until reduced by about one-half. Meanwhile, dissolve cornstarch in a little water. Whisk the cornstarch mixture into the boiling liquid. Boil, stirring, until the gravy thickens.

Winter Basics

DRIED FRUIT CHUTNEY

Before the advent of vacuum packaging, summer fruits were dried at the height of their season and used as pantry staples throughout the winter months. Use a few tablespoons of this ginger-laced preserve to complement roast chicken or pork chops. Other dried fruits—such as apples, pineapples, cherries and cranberries—can be substituted for those suggested here.

1   cup (7 oz/220 g) firmly packed brown sugar

1   cup (8 fl oz/250 ml) sherry vinegar

4   cups (32 fl oz/1 l) water

1   teaspoon finely grated lemon zest

¼   cup (2 fl oz/60 ml) fresh lemon juice

⅛   teaspoon cayenne pepper

1   teaspoon salt

2   cups (10 oz/315 g) dried figs, stems removed

2   cups (12 oz/375 g) dried apricots

1   cup (6 oz/185 g) pitted prunes

1   cup (6 oz/185 g) golden raisins (sultanas)

½   cup (1 oz/30 g) crystallized ginger, finely chopped

IN A SAUCEPAN over medium heat, combine the sugar, vinegar, water, lemon zest, lemon juice, cayenne and salt. Bring to a boil, reduce the heat to low and simmer, uncovered, until the mixture thickens slightly, about 20 minutes.

Add the figs, apricots, prunes, raisins and ginger and continue to cook, stirring occasionally, until the fruit is tender but not mushy and the syrup is thick, 1–1¼ hours. Add water during cooking if the mixture becomes dry. Remove from the heat.

Meanwhile, bring a large pot of water to a boil and immerse 6 half-pint (8-fl oz/250-ml) canning jars, lids and ring bands in the water. Boil for 15 minutes. Using tongs, remove the jars and place, upside down, on a kitchen towel to drain, then remove the lids and ring bands, placing them on the towel as well.

Ladle the chutney into the jars, filling to within ¼ inch (6 mm) of the rim. Wipe the rims with a clean, damp cloth. Seal tightly with sterilized lids and ring bands. Let cool on a kitchen towel away from any drafts. If the jars have sealed properly, the tops will not pop when pressed gently in the centers. Store in a cool, dark place for up to 1 year. Once opened (or if they have not sealed properly), store in the refrigerator for up to 1 month. *Makes 6 half-pint (8-fl oz/250-ml) jars*

SPICY CRANBERRY RELISH

This zesty relish is an ideal accompaniment to roast turkey or goose, or if an extra measure of chopped jalapeño is added, it makes a wonderful winter salsa with tortilla chips. If fresh cranberries are unavailable, frozen can be substituted with excellent results.

2   cups (8 oz/250 g) cranberries

¾   cup (4 oz/125 g) finely diced red (Spanish) onion

1   celery stalk, finely diced

1   large fresh jalapeño chili pepper, seeded and minced

5   tablespoons (2½ oz/75 g) sugar

1   teaspoon finely grated lime zest

3   tablespoons fresh lime juice

¼   cup (2 fl oz/60 ml) fresh orange juice

1   tablespoon peeled and grated fresh ginger

¼   cup (⅓ oz/10 g) chopped fresh mint

     salt and freshly ground pepper

PLACE THE CRANBERRIES in a food processor fitted with the metal blade and pulse to chop coarsely. Transfer to a bowl. Add the red onion, celery, jalapeño, sugar, lime zest, lime juice, orange juice, ginger and mint. Mix well and season to taste with salt and pepper. Cover and refrigerate until well chilled.

Serve chilled or store, tightly covered, in the refrigerator for up to 1 day. *Makes 2 cups (1¼ lb/625 g)*

HOT GINGER BUTTERED RUM

Nothing takes the chill off a cold winter's night like hot rum. Ginger-flavored brandy adds an extra touch of spice, although regular brandy will do in a pinch. Garnish each mug with a cinnamon stick.

⅓ cup (2½ oz/75 g) firmly packed brown sugar

4 cups (32 fl oz/1 l) water

¼ cup (2 oz/60 g) unsalted butter, cut into pieces

2 cinnamon sticks

6 whole cloves

¼ teaspoon freshly grated nutmeg

6 thin fresh ginger slices, each ¾ inch (2 cm) in diameter, peeled

¾ cup (6 fl oz/180 ml) dark rum

½ cup (4 fl oz/125 ml) ginger-flavored brandy

1 tablespoon fresh lemon juice

IN A SAUCEPAN over medium heat, stir together the brown sugar, water, butter, cinnamon sticks, cloves, nutmeg and ginger slices. Bring to a boil, reduce the heat to low and simmer for 5 minutes.

Remove from the heat and strain through a fine-mesh sieve into a warmed pitcher. Add the rum, brandy and lemon juice. Stir to mix.

Pour into warmed mugs and serve hot. *Makes about 5 cups (40 fl oz/1.25 l); serves 6*

ALL-SPICED CIDER

This drink is the perfect accompaniment to a holiday dessert buffet. Make a double batch, if you like, and store in the refrigerator; the flavor improves with age. To serve, simply warm the cider in a saucepan for several minutes until hot.

4½ cups (36 fl oz/1.1 l) apple cider

1 tablespoon light brown sugar

3 tablespoons fresh lemon juice

30 allspice berries

12 whole cloves

3 cinnamon sticks

¼ teaspoon freshly grated nutmeg

IN A SAUCEPAN, combine the cider, brown sugar, lemon juice, allspice berries, cloves, cinnamon sticks and nutmeg. Bring to a boil over high heat, reduce the heat to low and simmer for 5 minutes.

Remove from the heat and strain through a fine-mesh sieve into a warmed pitcher. Pour into warmed mugs and serve hot; or let cool, cover and refrigerate for up to 1 week. Before serving, warm over medium heat. *Makes about 5 cups (40 fl oz/1.25 l); serves 6*

BLOOD ORANGE MIMOSA

Winter's blood oranges bring refreshing taste and vibrant color to this sparkling aperitif. Don't use your best Champagne or sparkling wine; its nuances will be lost to the bold flavor of the juice.

1 fifth (24 fl oz/750 ml) Champagne or sparkling wine (*see note*)

  about 1½ cups (12 fl oz/375 ml) fresh blood orange juice

6 thin blood orange slices, each slit to the center

FILL CHAMPAGNE FLUTES halfway with Champagne or sparkling wine. Pour in enough blood orange juice to fill the glasses. Garnish the rim of each glass with a blood orange slice and serve at once.
Serves 6

openers

I taste a liquor never brewed,
From Tankards scooped in Pearl—

—Emily Dickinson

Oysters on the Half Shell with Mignonette Sauce

For the mignonette sauce:

½ cup (4 fl oz/125 ml) dry red wine such as Cabernet Sauvignon, Zinfandel or Pinot Noir

3–4 tablespoons red wine vinegar

4 shallots, minced

⅛ teaspoon red pepper flakes

freshly cracked black pepper

crushed or shaved ice

36 oysters in the shell

lemon wedges

flat-leaf (Italian) parsley sprigs

Folk wisdom holds that oysters may only be eaten safely during months with the letter *r* in their names. Although modern methods and standards for their cultivation now make them safe to eat year-round, the shellfish will be at their best in winter when the coastal waters from which they are harvested are at their coldest and freshest.

To make the mignonette sauce, in a small bowl, stir together the wine, 3 tablespoons vinegar, shallots, red pepper flakes and black pepper to taste. Taste and add more vinegar if needed.

Place the bowl of mignonette sauce on a platter and surround it with a bed of ice. Discard any oysters that do not close tightly to the touch. Scrub each oyster thoroughly with a stiff-bristled brush, rinsing it well under cold running water. Holding each oyster flat-side up in a kitchen towel and using an oyster knife, slip the tip of the knife into the shell near the hinge and pry upward to open. Run the knife blade along the inside of the top shell to sever the muscle that joins the shells, then lift off the top shell. Run the knife underneath the oyster to free it from the rounded, bottom shell, being careful not to spill the liquor. Nest the oysters in their shells on the ice.

Garnish the platter with lemon wedges and parsley sprigs and serve immediately. *Serves 6*

The bees are stirring—birds are on the wing—
And Winter slumbering in the open air,
Wears on his smiling face a dream of Spring!

—Samuel Taylor Coleridge

Spiced Shrimp Cigars

2	tablespoons olive oil
½	lb (250 g) medium shrimp (prawns), peeled and deveined
	salt and freshly ground pepper
¾	cup (4½ oz/140 g) peeled, seeded and chopped tomatoes (fresh or canned)
¼	cup (1½ oz/45 g) finely chopped yellow onion
2	cloves garlic, minced
3	tablespoons chopped fresh flat-leaf (Italian) parsley
¼	cup (⅓ oz/10 g) chopped fresh cilantro (fresh coriander)
1¼	teaspoons ground cumin
½	teaspoon sweet paprika
¼	teaspoon cayenne pepper
	pinch of saffron threads
	about ¼ cup (½ oz/15 g) fresh bread crumbs
9	sheets (about ½ lb/250 g) filo dough
2	tablespoons unsalted butter
2	tablespoons extra-virgin olive oil
	lemon wedges

These crispy finger-sized rolls are especially popular for entertaining during the holidays because they can be prepared up to 1 day in advance of serving: Simply shape the rolls, arrange them in a single layer on a baking sheet and refrigerate, then bake before serving.

IN A FRYING PAN over medium heat, warm the olive oil. Add the shrimp and cook, stirring occasionally, until they begin to turn pink, about 2 minutes. Season to taste with salt and pepper. Remove the pan from the heat and transfer the shrimp to a cutting board; chop coarsely and set aside.

Return the pan to medium-low heat. Add the tomatoes, onion, garlic, parsley, cilantro, cumin, paprika, cayenne and saffron and stir to mix well. Simmer slowly, stirring occasionally, until the moisture has evaporated, 5–10 minutes. Remove the pan from the heat and add the shrimp and enough bread crumbs to make a fairly dry mixture. Mix well and season to taste with salt and pepper.

Preheat an oven to 400°F (200°C). Lightly butter a baking sheet.

Place the filo sheets in a neat stack on a cutting board and cut the stack crosswise into quarters, forming strips about 4 inches (10 cm) wide. Cover with a dampened kitchen towel until ready to use.

In a small pan over medium heat, melt the butter with the extra-virgin olive oil. Remove from the heat. Brush 1 filo strip very lightly with the butter mixture and place a second strip on top. Brush the second strip lightly with the butter mixture. Place a heaping teaspoonful of filling along the short end nearest you. Fold in the sides of the filo to enclose the filling and then roll up to form a cigar shape. Place on the prepared baking sheet and brush lightly with the butter mixture. Repeat with remaining filo and filling.

Place the filo cigars on the prepared baking sheet. Bake until golden, about 15 minutes. Transfer to a platter and garnish with lemon wedges. Serve immediately. *Makes 18 rolls; serves 6*

For the blinis:

1   **cup (3½ oz/105 g) buck-wheat flour**

1   **cup (5 oz/155 g) all-purpose (plain) flour**

¼   **teaspoon salt**

1   **package (2½ teaspoons) active dry yeast**

3   **tablespoons plus ¾ cup (6 fl oz/180 ml) lukewarm water (110°F/43°C)**

2   **tablespoons sugar**

1¾   **cups (14 fl oz/430 ml) milk**

3   **eggs, beaten**

¼   **cup (2 oz/60 g) unsalted butter, melted**

    vegetable oil

For the topping:

6   **oz (185 g) thinly sliced smoked salmon**

1   **cup (8 fl oz/250 ml) sour cream**

1   **oz (30 g) good-quality caviar**

    small fresh dill sprigs

Buckwheat Blinis with Smoked Salmon and Caviar

Blinis, yeasted miniature buckwheat pancakes, are perfect vehicles for eating smoked salmon and caviar. They originated in Russia, where they were traditionally served with sour cream and salt herring.

TO MAKE THE BLINIS, sift together the buckwheat flour, all-purpose flour and salt into a bowl. In a small bowl, combine the yeast, the 3 tablespoons lukewarm water, 1 tablespoon of the sugar and ¼ cup (2 oz/60 g) of the flour mixture; stir to mix well. Cover with plastic wrap and let stand in a warm place (75°F/24°C) until bubbly, about 30 minutes.

In a large bowl, whisk together 1 cup (8 fl oz/250 ml) of the milk, the remaining ¾ cup (6 fl oz/180 ml) water, the eggs, butter and the remaining 1 tablespoon sugar. Stir in the yeast mixture and enough of the remaining flour mixture to make a batter the consistency of sour cream. Cover the bowl with plastic wrap and let the dough rise in a warm place until the mixture is frothy and doubled in volume, about 30 minutes.

In a small saucepan, warm the remaining ¾ cup (6 fl oz/180 ml) milk until bubbles form around the edges of the pan. Pour the milk into the batter. Mix well.

Place a large frying pan over medium heat and add about 1 teaspoon vegetable oil. Tilt the pan to coat the bottom with the oil. When the oil is hot, using a tablespoon, drop the batter onto the pan; do not crowd the pan. Using the back of the spoon, spread each spoonful of batter to make a round 2½–3 inches (6–7.5 cm) in diameter. Cook until bubbles appear on the surface and then break, about 10 seconds. Turn and cook on the second sides until lightly golden, 10–15 seconds longer. Transfer to a warmed plate and keep warm while you cook the remaining batter. You should have 32–36 blinis in all.

To serve, place the blinis on a warmed serving plate. Top each blini with a piece of the smoked salmon, a small spoonful of sour cream, a tiny mound of caviar and a tiny sprig of dill. *Serves 6*

3   **lb (1.5 kg) mussels, debearded and well scrubbed**

2   **tablespoons extra-virgin olive oil**

1   **small red (Spanish) onion, chopped**

4   **cloves garlic, minced**

3   **cups (24 fl oz/750 ml) dry red wine such as Cabernet Sauvignon, Zinfandel or Pinot Noir**

2   **tablespoons coarsely chopped fresh flat-leaf (Italian) parsley, plus parsley sprigs for garnish**

1   **teaspoon chopped fresh thyme**

½   **teaspoon chopped fresh winter savory, optional**

3   **bay leaves**

    salt and freshly ground pepper

Steamed Mussels with Garlic and Herbs

Mussels are available almost year-round but are at their peak from November through March. Avoid those with broken shells, open shells, or ones that feel heavy compared to their size, and use them the same day they are purchased. Serve this dish as a satisfying first course, or even as a main course with plenty of crusty bread and a garden salad.

DISCARD ANY MUSSELS that do not close to the touch. In a large frying pan over medium-low heat, warm the olive oil. Add the onion and sauté until soft, about 10 minutes. Add the garlic and cook, stirring constantly, for 1 minute. Pour in the red wine and add the mussels, chopped parsley, thyme, savory (if using) and bay leaves. Cover and simmer until the mussels open, 3–5 minutes. Check the mussels periodically; as they open, transfer them to a serving bowl and cover to keep warm. Discard any that have not opened. When all of the mussels have been removed from the pan, uncover and reduce the cooking liquid over high heat by one-fourth, 2–4 minutes. Discard the bay leaves. Season to taste with salt and pepper.

Pour the reduced pan sauce over the mussels and garnish with parsley sprigs. Serve immediately. *Serves 6*

1 teaspoon olive oil

½ lb (250 g) fresh salmon fillet,
about ¾ inch (2 cm) thick,
skin and any errant bones
removed

salt and freshly ground
pepper

6 oz (185 g) smoked salmon,
coarsely chopped

3–4 teaspoons fresh lemon juice

3 tablespoons mayonnaise

3 tablespoons chopped fresh
dill

2 tablespoons well-drained
capers, chopped

½ baguette, cut on the diagonal
into thin slices and lightly
toasted

2 tablespoons snipped fresh
chives

thin lemon slices, optional

Two-Way Salmon Toasts

These toasts are a perfect hors d'oeuvre to serve on New Year's Eve with
Champagne. You can make the salmon spread several hours in advance and
store it in the refrigerator; spread it on the toasts just before serving.

IN A NONSTICK FRYING PAN over medium heat, warm the olive oil. Add the
fresh salmon and cook on the first side for 3 minutes. Turn, season to taste
with salt and pepper and continue to cook until the salmon is opaque
throughout, 3–4 minutes longer. Remove from the heat and let cool.

Chop the cooked salmon coarsely and place it in a large bowl. Add the
smoked salmon, 3 teaspoons lemon juice, mayonnaise, dill and capers. Taste
and add more lemon juice if needed.

To serve, spread the salmon on the toasts, dividing it evenly. Garnish with
the chives and lemon slices, if desired. Serve immediately. *Serves 6*

Fish say, they have their own stream and pond.

But is there anything beyond?

—Rupert Brooke

Smoked Trout in Endive Spears

¼	cup (2 fl oz/60 ml) mayonnaise
6	green (spring) onions, including 1 inch (2.5 cm) of the tender greens, thinly sliced
2	small cloves garlic, minced
1½	teaspoons fresh lemon juice
⅛	teaspoon cayenne pepper
½	teaspoon sweet paprika
	salt and freshly ground pepper
1½	cups (7½ oz/235 g) flaked smoked trout fillet
4	heads Belgian endive (chicory/witloof)
	lemon wedges

Although long a common ingredient in the kitchens of Belgium and France, Belgian endive did not gain favor in America until the 1970s, when it became a favorite addition to salads. The leaves of the compact head are tender and crisp and the flavor ranges from sweet to bitter. Peak season runs from November to April.

IN A SMALL BOWL, combine the mayonnaise, green onions, garlic, lemon juice, cayenne, paprika and salt and pepper to taste. Mix well. Add the trout and stir to combine.

Cut off the base from each endive and separate the heads into individual spears. Use only the larger endive spears; reserve the smaller ones for another use.

Using the broad end of each spear, scoop up a heaping teaspoonful of the trout mixture, then spread it along the spears with a knife. Arrange on a platter and garnish with lemon wedges. Serve immediately. *Serves 6*

May the countryside and the gliding valley streams content me.
Lost to fame, let me love river and woodland.

—Virgil

Pâté de Campagne

6	slices bacon
3	tablespoons unsalted butter
1	lb (500 g) calf's liver, trimmed of any membranes, cut into 2-inch (5-cm) pieces
1	lb (500 g) chicken livers, trimmed of any membranes
1	lb (500 g) ground (minced) pork
5	green (spring) onions, coarsely chopped
2	eggs
2	tablespoons all-purpose (plain) flour
2	tablespoons Cognac or other good-quality brandy
6	cloves garlic, minced
2	tablespoons chopped fresh thyme
2	teaspoons chopped fresh oregano
1	tablespoon salt
1½	teaspoons ground allspice
½	teaspoon freshly grated nutmeg
½	teaspoon freshly ground pepper
4	bay leaves
	boiling water, as needed

To give the rich flavors of this country pâté time to mingle, make it up to 1 week in advance, refrigerating it tightly wrapped in plastic wrap. Serve with crackers or crusty bread, mustard, cornichons and caper berries.

BRING A SAUCEPAN three-fourths full of water to a boil. Add the bacon, reduce the heat to low and simmer for 10 minutes. Drain. Set the bacon aside.

In a large frying pan over medium heat, melt the butter. Add the calf's liver and chicken livers and cook, stirring constantly, until the livers are barely firm to the touch and the centers are still pink, about 3 minutes. Transfer the livers and their juices to a food processor fitted with the metal blade. Process to a rough paste, 45–60 seconds. Transfer to a large bowl.

Place the pork and green onions in the food processor and process to a paste, 45–60 seconds. Add to the bowl containing the liver along with the eggs, flour, Cognac or brandy, garlic, thyme, oregano, salt, allspice, nutmeg and pepper. Stir until blended.

Preheat an oven to 350°F (180°C).

Place 3 strips of bacon lengthwise in a 9-by-5-inch (23-by-13-cm) loaf pan. Spoon the pâté mixture into the pan and arrange the bay leaves decoratively on top. Cover with the remaining bacon strips. Cover the pan tightly with aluminum foil, set the pan in a larger baking pan and place in the oven. Pour boiling water into the larger pan to a depth of 1 inch (2.5 cm). Bake until the juices run clear when the pâté is pierced with a knife, about 1 hour and 40 minutes. Remove the loaf pan from the water bath and transfer to a rack. Remove the foil and let cool on the rack for about 30 minutes.

Cover the cooled pâté with waxed paper and place a 2-lb (1-kg) weight on top. Refrigerate, weighted, for at least 1 day or for up to 1 week.

To serve, invert the pâté onto a cutting board, lift off the pan and discard the bacon. Cut into thin slices, then cut each slice in half and arrange on a serving plate. Serve at room temperature. *Serves 12–14*

soups
and stews

Wild Mushroom Soup with Blue Cheese Toasts

For the soup:

2½ tablespoons unsalted butter

1   yellow onion, chopped

1   lb (500 g) fresh button mushrooms, brushed clean and coarsely chopped

1   oz (30 g) dried porcini mushrooms

6   cups (48 fl oz/1.5 l) chicken stock

4   cups (32 fl oz/1 l) water

½   lb (250 g) fresh wild mushrooms *(see note)*, brushed clean and thinly sliced

    salt and freshly ground pepper

½   cup (4 fl oz/125 ml) heavy (double) cream

1   tablespoon fresh lemon juice

For the blue cheese toasts:

2   oz (60 g) blue cheese such as Roquefort, Stilton or Gorgonzola, at room temperature

1½ teaspoons unsalted butter, at room temperature

    salt and freshly ground pepper

6   baguette slices, lightly toasted

2   tablespoons finely snipped fresh chives

A warm bowl of this soup is a welcome treat in the cold depths of winter. The fresh wild mushrooms preferred for this recipe are porcini, hedgehogs, chanterelles or shiitakes; if unavailable, substitute fresh button mushrooms.

TO MAKE THE SOUP, in a large soup pot over medium-high heat, melt 1½ tablespoons of the butter. Add the onion and cook, stirring occasionally, until soft, about 10 minutes. Raise the heat to high, add the button mushrooms, dried porcini mushrooms, stock and water and bring to a boil. Reduce the heat to medium-low and simmer, uncovered, until the mushrooms are tender, about 30 minutes. Remove from the heat and let cool for about 15 minutes.

Meanwhile, in a frying pan over medium-high heat, melt the remaining 1 tablespoon butter. Add the sliced wild mushrooms and sauté, stirring occasionally, until the mushrooms are soft and the mushroom liquid has evaporated, 6–8 minutes. Season to taste with salt and pepper. Transfer to a dish and set aside.

Using a blender and working in batches, purée the soup until smooth, 3–4 minutes for each batch. Strain through a fine-mesh sieve into a clean soup pot. Add the cream and sautéed wild mushrooms and stir to combine. Stir in the lemon juice and season to taste with salt and pepper. Place over medium heat and reheat to serving temperature.

To make the toasts, in a small bowl, mash together the blue cheese and butter. Season to taste with salt and pepper. Spread the cheese onto the toasted baguette slices and place on an ungreased baking sheet. Broil (grill) until the cheese is bubbling around the edges, 30–60 seconds. Remove from the broiler and sprinkle with the chives.

To serve, ladle the soup into warmed bowls and float a blue cheese toast in the center of each bowl. Serve immediately. *Serves 6*

There's no getting blood out of a turnip.

—Captain Frederick Marryat

Beef Stew with Turnips

¼ cup (2 fl oz/60 ml) olive oil

2 yellow onions, finely chopped

2 oz (60 g) bacon or pancetta, finely diced

3 lb (1.5 kg) beef stew meat such as chuck roast or sirloin tip, cut into 1–1½-inch (2½–4-cm) cubes

¼ cup (1½ oz/45 g) all-purpose (plain) flour

4 cloves garlic, minced

6 fresh parsley stems

2 fresh thyme sprigs

2 bay leaves

1½ cups (12 fl oz/375 ml) dry red wine such as Cabernet Sauvignon or Côtes-du-Rhône

3 cups (24 fl oz/750 ml) beef or veal stock

1 tablespoon tomato paste

4 turnips or 15 baby turnips, peeled and larger ones cut into wedges

1 bunch (about 10 oz/315 g) turnip greens, stems removed and leaves cut crosswise into strips

salt and freshly ground pepper

Turnips have a delicately sweet flavor when young, but as they mature they lose their sweetness and become woody. Therefore, it is best to buy them when they are at their peak, between November and February. The greens, which are edible, should be bright green and garden fresh. If unavailable, substitute Swiss chard (silverbeet), dandelion greens, beet greens or kale.

IN A LARGE, HEAVY POT over medium heat, warm the olive oil. Add the onions and bacon or pancetta, and sauté until the onions are soft, about 10 minutes. Using a slotted spoon, transfer the onions and bacon or pancetta to a plate and set aside.

Working in batches, add the beef to the pot in a single layer; do not crowd the pot. Cook uncovered, turning occasionally, until golden brown on all sides, 7–10 minutes. When all the meat is browned, return it to the pot, sprinkle with the flour and cook, stirring, until the meat is evenly coated, about 1 minute. Return the onions and bacon or pancetta to the pot and add the garlic. Using kitchen string, tie the parsley stems, thyme sprigs and bay leaves into a bundle and add to the pot as well.

Raise the heat to high, pour in the wine and bring to a boil, stirring to scrape up any browned bits from the pot bottom. Reduce the heat to medium and simmer, stirring occasionally, until the liquid is reduced by one-fourth, 3–5 minutes. Add the stock and tomato paste and stir well. Bring to a boil over high heat, then reduce the heat to low, cover and simmer until the meat is tender when pierced with a knife, 1½–2 hours.

Remove the herb bundle and discard. Add the turnips, cover and cook until tender when pierced with a fork, about 15 minutes. Add the turnip greens, cover and cook until wilted, about 2 minutes. Season to taste with salt and pepper.

To serve, ladle the stew into warmed bowls and serve at once. *Serves 6*

Parsnip and Carrot Soup

1½   tablespoons unsalted butter

1   yellow onion, chopped

1¼   lb (625 g) parsnips, peeled
     and coarsely chopped

1   lb (500 g) carrots, peeled and
     coarsely chopped

6   cups (48 fl oz/1.5 l) chicken
     stock

4   cups (32 fl oz/1 l) water
     salt and freshly ground
     pepper

For the yogurt garnish:

⅓   cup (3 oz/90 g) plain yogurt

     about 2 tablespoons milk

     salt and freshly ground
     pepper

1½   tablespoons chopped fresh
     flat-leaf (Italian) parsley

Introduced to the United States from Europe in the early seventeenth century, the parsnip is a creamy white root vegetable similar in shape and sweetness to the carrot. The wintertime chill turns the parsnip's natural starch to sugar, giving it its distinctive sweetness. Look for parsnips that are small to medium; larger ones can have a coarse texture.

IN A LARGE SOUP POT over medium heat, melt the butter. Add the onion and sauté, stirring occasionally, until soft, about 10 minutes. Raise the heat to high, add the parsnips, carrots, stock and water and bring to a boil. Reduce the heat to medium-low and simmer, uncovered, until the vegetables are tender, about 30 minutes.

Using a blender and working in batches, purée the soup on high speed until smooth, 3–4 minutes for each batch. Strain through a fine-mesh sieve into a clean soup pot. Place over low heat and reheat to serving temperature. Season to taste with salt and pepper.

While the soup is heating, make the yogurt garnish: In a small bowl, whisk together the yogurt and enough milk to make a barely fluid paste. Season to taste with salt and pepper.

To serve, ladle the soup into warmed bowls and drizzle with the yogurt. Sprinkle with the parsley and serve immediately. *Serves 6*

If Leeks you like, but do their smell dislike,
Eat Onyons, and you shall not smell the Leeke…

—William Kitchiner

Three-Onion Soup

3	tablespoons extra-virgin olive oil
4	large yellow onions, diced
4	leeks, including 1 inch (2.5 cm) of the tender greens, carefully rinsed and diced
3	oz (90 g) pancetta, finely diced
5	cloves garlic, minced
6	cups (48 fl oz/1.5 l) chicken stock
1¼	cups (10 fl oz/310 ml) fruity red wine such as Chianti or Zinfandel
2	tablespoons balsamic vinegar
1	tablespoon red wine vinegar
	salt and freshly ground pepper
¾	cup (3 oz/90 g) freshly grated Parmesan cheese

Yellow onions, leeks and garlic are the three onion family members combined in this full-flavored soup. For a heartier rendition, toast slices of country-style bread on both sides until golden and rub them on one side with whole garlic cloves. Place a slice of bread in the bottom of each soup bowl and ladle the hot soup over the bread.

IN A SOUP POT over medium heat, warm the olive oil. Add the onions, leeks and pancetta and sauté, stirring occasionally, until the onions and leeks are soft, about 10 minutes. Add the garlic and sauté, stirring, for 1 minute. Add the stock and simmer, uncovered, over medium-low heat, until the vegetables are very soft, about 30 minutes.

Just before serving, stir in the red wine, balsamic vinegar and red wine vinegar. Season to taste with salt and pepper. Place over low heat and reheat to serving temperature.

To serve, ladle the soup into warmed bowls. Sprinkle the Parmesan cheese equally over each serving and serve at once. *Serves 6*

Simple Simon met a pieman
Going to the fair:
Says Simple Simon to the pieman,
"Let me taste your ware."

—Nursery Rhyme

Chicken Pot Pie

For the pie filling:

1   chicken, 3½ lb (1.75 kg), cut into 8 pieces and skinned

1   teaspoon chopped fresh thyme

2   bay leaves

7   cups (56 fl oz/1.75 l) chicken stock or water

½   lb (250 g) pearl onions

¼   cup (2 oz/60 g) unsalted butter

⅓   cup (2 oz/60 g) all-purpose (plain) flour

3   carrots, peeled and cut into 1-inch (2.5-cm) pieces

2   celery stalks, cut into 1-inch (2.5-cm) pieces

¾   lb (375 g) red potatoes, un-peeled, quartered lengthwise

1   cup (5 oz/155 g) green peas

¾   lb (375 g) fresh button mush-rooms, halved

     salt and freshly ground pepper

For the biscuits:

2½   cups (12½ oz/390 g) all-pur-pose (plain) flour sifted with ¾ teaspoon salt and 1 table-spoon baking powder

½   cup (4 oz/125 g) unsalted butter, cut into pieces, at room temperature

¾   cup (6 fl oz/180 ml) butter-milk, at room temperature

5   green (spring) onions, sliced

TO MAKE THE FILLING, in a soup pot over high heat, combine the chicken, thyme, bay leaves and stock or water. Bring to a boil, reduce the heat to low and simmer, uncovered, until the chicken is tender, about 45 minutes.

Meanwhile, peel the pearl onions: Bring a saucepan half full of water to a boil. Add the onions and boil for 2 minutes. Drain, rinse with cold water, and drain again. Trim off the root ends, then cut a shallow X into each trimmed end. Slip off the skins. Set aside.

Remove the soup pot from the heat. Using a slotted spoon, remove the chicken and set aside until cool enough to handle. Discard the bay leaves. Remove the meat from the bones and cut into 1-inch (2.5-cm) pieces. Using a large spoon, skim the fat from the top of the broth. Reserve the broth (about 5 cups/40 fl oz/1.25 l) and chicken separately.

In a saucepan over low heat, melt the butter. Add the flour and stir for 1 minute. Whisk in the reserved broth, bring to a boil over medium-high heat and boil until thickened, about 2 minutes. Reduce the heat to medium-low and add the carrots, celery, pearl onions and potatoes. Cook until the vegetables are tender, about 25 minutes. Add the chicken, peas and mushrooms and cook until the mushrooms are tender, about 5 minutes. Season with salt and pepper. Transfer to a 3½-qt (3.5-l) round baking dish 7–8 inches (18–20 cm) in diameter.

Preheat an oven to 425°F (220°C). To make the biscuits, place the sifted mix-ture in a bowl. Using your fingers, rub in the butter until the mixture resembles coarse meal. Using a fork, mix in the buttermilk and green onions and form into a ball. Transfer to a floured work surface and roll out into a round ½ inch (12 mm) thick. Fold in half and roll it out again. Repeat this step a third time. Using a round biscuit cutter 2 inches (5 cm) in diameter, cut out 12 biscuits.

Place the biscuits, evenly spaced and touching slightly, on the chicken mix-ture. Bake until the biscuits are golden and the stew is bubbling, 25–35 minutes. Spoon into warmed bowls and serve hot. *Serves 6*

Food and beauty are human nature.

—Confucius

Jerusalem Artichoke Soup with Hazelnut-Orange Butter

3   tablespoons unsalted butter

3   celery stalks with leaves, diced

3   large yellow onions, diced

2½ teaspoons ground coriander

3   lb (1.5 kg) Jerusalem artichokes, unpeeled, cut into 1-inch (2.5-cm) pieces

2   orange zest strips, each 3 inches (7.5 cm) long and ¾ inch (2 cm) wide

9   cups (2¼ qt/2.25 l) chicken stock

For the hazelnut-orange butter:

¼   cup (1¼ oz/37 g) hazelnuts (filberts)

1   teaspoon grated orange zest

2   tablespoons unsalted butter, at room temperature

    salt and freshly ground pepper

3   tablespoons fresh orange juice

    salt and freshly ground pepper

Native to North America, Jerusalem artichokes are members of the sunflower family. The sweet tubers, which resemble fresh ginger and have a taste similar to artichokes, possess a rich, creamy consistency that lends itself to soups.

IN A LARGE SOUP POT over medium heat, melt the butter. Add the celery and onions and sauté, stirring occasionally, until the vegetables are soft, about 10 minutes. Add the coriander and sauté, stirring, for 1 minute longer. Add the Jerusalem artichokes, orange zest and chicken stock and bring to a boil over high heat. Reduce the heat to medium-low and simmer, uncovered, until the Jerusalem artichokes are soft, about 30 minutes.

Meanwhile, make the butter: Preheat an oven to 350°F (180°C). Spread the hazelnuts on a baking sheet and toast in the oven until lightly browned and fragrant, 5–7 minutes. Remove from the oven and, while the nuts are still warm, place in a kitchen towel and rub to remove the skins. Do not worry if bits of skin remain. Let cool, then finely chop the nuts and place in a small bowl with the orange zest and butter. Using a fork, mash together well. Season to taste with salt and pepper. Cover and chill for 15 minutes. Using a teaspoon, divide the butter into 6 equal portions, forming each into a ball. Flatten each ball slightly and place them on a plate. Cover and refrigerate until needed.

When the Jerusalem artichokes are soft, remove from the heat and let cool slightly. Remove the orange zest and discard. Using a blender and working in batches, purée the soup on high speed until smooth, 3–4 minutes for each batch. Strain the purée through a fine-mesh sieve into a clean saucepan. Add the orange juice and mix well. Season to taste with salt and pepper.

To serve, place the soup over medium heat and reheat to serving temperature. Ladle the soup into warmed bowls and place a piece of the hazelnut-orange butter in the center of each serving. Serve at once. *Serves 6*

Here are sweet peas, on tip-toe for a flight.

—John Keats

Split Pea Soup

2   smoked ham hocks (about ¾ lb/375 g each)

1½   cups (10½ oz/330 g) yellow or orange split peas

2   tablespoons unsalted butter

1   yellow onion, coarsely chopped

1   carrot, peeled and coarsely chopped

8   cups (64 fl oz/2 l) chicken stock, vegetable stock or water, plus extra as needed

     salt and freshly ground pepper

     coarsely chopped fresh flat-leaf (Italian) parsley

Dried peas and beans have long been menu standards of the winter months. Richly flavored split peas paired with smoked ham hocks is a classic cold-weather combination. Top with buttery croutons before serving, if you like.

BRING A LARGE SAUCEPAN three-fourths full of water to a boil. Add the ham hocks and simmer for 1 minute. Drain and set aside.

Pick over the split peas and discard any damaged peas or impurities. Rinse the peas and drain.

In a soup pot over medium heat, melt the butter. Add the onion and carrot and sauté, stirring occasionally, until the vegetables are soft, about 10 minutes. Add the ham hocks, split peas and stock or water. Bring to a boil, reduce the heat to low and simmer gently until the peas are soft, 50–60 minutes.

Remove from the heat. Remove the ham hocks and let stand until cool enough to handle. Let the soup cool slightly.

Using a blender and working in batches, purée the soup on high speed until smooth, about 2 minutes for each batch. Return the purée to a clean soup pot and thin with more stock or water, if needed. Place over medium heat and reheat to serving temperature. Season to taste with salt and pepper.

While the soup is heating, remove the meat from the ham hocks and discard the skin and bones. Cut the meat into small pieces and add to the soup. Stir to heat through.

To serve, ladle the soup into warmed bowls and garnish with parsley. Serve hot. *Serves 6*

O, wind,

If Winter comes, can Spring be far behind?

—Percy Bysshe Shelley

Vegetarian Black Bean Chili

- 2¼ **cups (1 lb/500 g) dried black beans**
- 3 **tablespoons olive oil**
- 3 **yellow onions, chopped**
- 2 **fresh serrano or jalapeño chili peppers, seeded and minced**
- 5 **large cloves garlic, minced**
- 6 **tablespoons (1 oz/30 g) chili powder**
- 3 **tablespoons ground cumin**
- ¼ **teaspoon cayenne pepper**
- 1 **teaspoon dried oregano**
- 2 **cans (28 oz/875 g each) crushed tomatoes**

   salt and freshly ground pepper
- 1 **cup (4 oz/125 g) coarsely grated Monterey Jack cheese**

Dried beans are an age-old pantry staple of this time of year and nearly any variety will work well in this recipe; some good choices include navy beans, cannellini beans or red beans. If you like, garnish with sour cream and chopped fresh cilantro (fresh coriander).

PICK OVER THE BEANS and discard any damaged beans or impurities. Rinse the beans. Place in a bowl and add water to cover generously. Let soak for about 3 hours. Drain the beans and set aside.

In a large, heavy saucepan over low heat, warm the olive oil. Add the onions and chili peppers and sauté, stirring occasionally, until the onions are soft, about 10 minutes. Add the garlic, chili powder, cumin, cayenne and oregano and sauté, stirring, for 2 minutes longer. Add the beans, tomatoes and water to cover by 3 inches (7.5 cm). Bring to a boil over high heat. Reduce the heat to low and simmer, uncovered, until the beans are very tender and have begun to fall apart, 2½–3 hours. Add water if the beans begin to dry out but are not yet cooked.

Season to taste with salt and pepper. Ladle into warmed bowls, sprinkle with the cheese and serve at once. *Serves 6*

When all aloud the wind doth blow...
When roasted crabs hiss in the bowl.

—William Shakespeare

2   Dungeness crabs, 1–1½ lb
    (500–750 g) each, cooked

2   tablespoons unsalted butter

1   small yellow onion, chopped

1   carrot, peeled and coarsely
    chopped

1   celery stalk, coarsely
    chopped

1½ cups (9 oz/280 g) chopped
    tomatoes (fresh or canned)

1½ cups (12 fl oz/375 ml) dry
    white wine such as
    Sauvignon Blanc

1   tablespoon chopped fresh
    tarragon, optional

¼   cup (1¼ oz/37 g) all-purpose
    (plain) flour

3   cups (24 fl oz/750 ml) bottled
    clam juice

3   cups (24 fl oz/750 ml) water

1   cup (8 fl oz/250 ml) heavy
    (double) cream

1   tablespoon Cognac or other
    good-quality brandy

    pinch of cayenne pepper

    salt and freshly ground
    pepper

Crab Bisque

Although Dungeness crabs provide the most meat, any variety—such as king, snow or blue crabs—may be used in this traditional bisque.

FIRST, CLEAN AND CRACK the crabs: Twist off the legs and claws and set aside. Place each crab on its back and pull off the small triangular apron-shaped shell flap, then insert your thumb underneath the top shell and pull it off. Remove the dark gray intestines and the feather-shaped white spongy gills from the body and discard. Rinse the crab body well. Break the body in half and remove the meat from the cavities. Using a mallet, crack the legs in several places and remove the meat. Set aside the crab meat in a bowl. Crack the large claws and carefully remove the meat from each claw in a single piece. Slice the meat and set aside for garnish. Using kitchen shears, cut the shells into small pieces; set aside.

In a saucepan over low heat, melt the butter. Add the onion, carrot and celery and sauté, stirring occasionally, until the vegetables are soft, about 15 minutes. Add the crab shells, tomatoes, wine and tarragon. Sprinkle the flour over the top and stir to mix well. Bring to a boil, reduce the heat to low, cover and simmer for 20 minutes. Remove from the heat and let cool slightly.

In a bowl, combine the clam juice and water. Combine one-third of the clam juice mixture and one-third of the shell mixture in a blender. Pulse briefly to break up the shells. Place a fine-mesh sieve lined with cheesecloth (muslin) over a bowl. Pour the contents of the blender through the sieve. Repeat with the remaining clam juice and shell mixtures in 2 batches. Transfer to a clean soup pot.

Place the pot over low heat and bring to a gentle simmer. Stir in the cream, brandy and cayenne and season to taste with salt and pepper. Add the reserved crab meat and heat through. Ladle into warmed bowls and garnish with the claw meat. Serve immediately. *Serves 6*

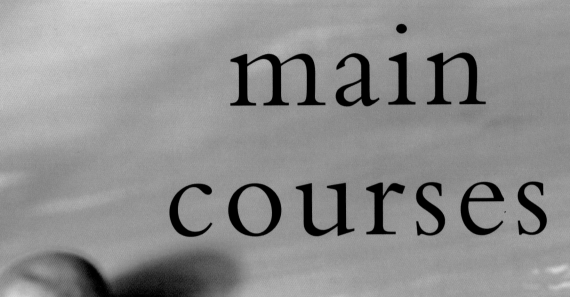

main
courses

3	lb (1.5 kg) store-bought sauerkraut, uncooked
2	tablespoons unsalted butter
2	yellow onions, minced
4	slices bacon, diced
2	bay leaves
4	whole cloves
20	juniper berries
2	cloves garlic, minced
2	cups (16 fl oz/500 ml) fruity white wine, preferably Riesling or Gewürztraminer
2	cups (16 fl oz/500 ml) chicken stock
8	pork sausages or 1 kielbasa sausage, about 2 lb (1 kg) total
2	lb (1 kg) red potatoes, unpeeled, cut into 1½-inch (4-cm) pieces
	salt and freshly ground pepper

Choucroute Garnie

Choucroute is French for "sauerkraut." This stick-to-your-ribs dish is made with much enthusiasm in the northeastern French region of Alsace. Served with beer or the same wine used in the dish, choucroute satisfies the soul on a cold winter's night. Serve with good country-style rye bread and plenty of hot mustard for the sausage.

PLACE THE SAUERKRAUT in a large colander and rinse well with cold running water. Drain well and set aside.

In a large, heavy pot over medium-low heat, melt the butter. Add the onions and bacon and sauté, stirring occasionally, until the onions are soft, about 10 minutes. Add the bay leaves, cloves, juniper berries, garlic, wine, stock and sauerkraut. Raise the heat to high and bring to a boil. Reduce the heat to low, cover and simmer gently until the sauerkraut is tender and the flavors have blended, 2–2½ hours.

Prick the pork sausage or kielbasa all over with a fork and add to the pot along with the potatoes. Cover and continue to simmer until the potatoes are tender, about 30 minutes longer. Season to taste with salt and pepper.

To serve, remove the pork sausages or kielbasa from the pot and cut into slices. Return to the pot and mix well. Spoon the sauerkraut, sausages and potatoes onto a warmed platter and serve hot. *Serves 6*

Roast Goose with Apple, Pear and Cranberry Stuffing

For the goose:

1   **goose, 9–10 lb (4.5–5 kg)**

    salt and freshly ground pepper

1   **cup (4 oz/125 g) dried cranberries**

¾   **cup (6 fl oz/180 ml) port wine**

1   **cup (8 fl oz/250 ml) chicken stock**

2   **tablespoons unsalted butter**

1   **small red (Spanish) onion, diced**

4   **Granny Smith or pippin apples, peeled, halved, cored and cut into 1-inch (2.5-cm) pieces**

3   **Bosc pears, peeled, halved, cored and cut into 1-inch (2.5-cm) pieces**

1   **tablespoon chopped fresh sage**

2   **teaspoons chopped fresh thyme**

½   **teaspoon ground cinnamon**

1   **cup (4 oz/125 g) fine dried bread crumbs**

    boiling water, as needed

For the pan gravy (optional):

1½   **cups (12 fl oz/375 ml) chicken stock**

1   **teaspoon cornstarch (cornflour) blended with 2 tablespoons water**

RINSE THE GOOSE under cold water, drain and pat dry with paper towels. Season the cavity and the outside skin of the bird with salt and pepper.

In a saucepan over low heat, combine the cranberries, port and stock. Bring to a simmer, cover and simmer gently until the cranberries are tender and about ¼ cup (2 fl oz/60 ml) liquid remains, about 10 minutes. Set aside.

Preheat an oven to 425°F (220°C). In a large frying pan over medium heat, melt the butter. Add the onion and cook, stirring occasionally, until soft, about 10 minutes. Add the apples and pears, cover and cook, stirring occasionally, until the fruits are tender but retain their shape, 10–12 minutes. Transfer to a bowl. Add the cranberries and their liquid, sage, thyme, cinnamon and bread crumbs and stir together. Season to taste with salt and pepper.

Prick the skin around the thighs, back and lower breast of the goose. Stuff loosely with the stuffing, then truss as directed on page 15. Place, breast-side up, on an oiled rack in a roasting pan. Roast for 15 minutes. Reduce the heat to 350°F (180°C) and continue to roast, basting with 3 tablespoons boiling water every 20 minutes, until the juices run a pale yellow when the thickest part of the thigh is pierced or an instant-read thermometer inserted into the thickest part of the thigh away from the bone registers 180°F (82°C), about 2½ hours longer. Transfer the goose to a serving platter. Cover loosely with aluminum foil and let stand for 15 minutes before carving.

Meanwhile, make the pan gravy, if using: Pour off the fat from the roasting pan and place the pan over high heat. Pour in the stock and deglaze the pan by stirring to dislodge any browned bits from the pan bottom. Boil until reduced by half, 2–3 minutes. Whisk in the cornstarch mixture and boil until thickened slightly, about 1 minute longer. Strain into a warmed sauceboat.

Snip the trussing string. Spoon the stuffing into a warmed serving bowl. Carve the goose at the table. Serve with the gravy, if using. *Serves 6–8*

Butternut Squash and Bacon Risotto

⅓   cup (1½ oz/45 g) hazelnuts (filberts) or pecans

1   butternut squash, 2–3 lb (1–1.5 kg)

4½ tablespoons olive oil

    salt and freshly ground pepper

4½ cups (36 fl oz/1.1 l) chicken stock

4½ cups (36 fl oz/1.1 l) water

3   slices bacon, finely diced

1   yellow onion, finely chopped

1½ teaspoons chopped fresh thyme

1½ teaspoons chopped fresh sage

¾   teaspoon chopped fresh rosemary

1¾ cups (12½ oz/390 g) Arborio rice

1   cup (4 oz/125 g) freshly grated Parmesan cheese

Butternut squash, a camel-colored, pear-shaped winter squash, is harvested in the fall but will keep well for several months in a cool, dry place. Other winter squash varieties—Hubbard, acorn, turban, buttercup—can be substituted.

PREHEAT AN OVEN to 375°F (190°C). Spread the nuts on a baking sheet and toast until lightly browned and fragrant, 5–7 minutes. Remove from the oven and let cool. Chop coarsely and set aside.

Peel the squash and cut lengthwise into 8 wedges. Scoop out the seeds and discard, then cut crosswise into thin slices. In a large frying pan over medium heat, warm 1½ tablespoons of the olive oil. Add the squash, cover and cook, turning occasionally, until almost tender, 7–10 minutes. Season to taste with salt and pepper and set aside. Meanwhile, in a saucepan, combine the stock and water and bring to a gentle simmer over medium heat.

In a large saucepan over medium heat, warm the remaining 3 tablespoons olive oil. Add the bacon and onion and sauté until the onion is soft, about 10 minutes. Add the thyme, sage, rosemary and rice and cook, stirring constantly, until the rice is translucent around the edges, 2–3 minutes. Add approximately ½ cup (4 fl oz/125 ml) of the simmering stock-water mixture and stir to scrape the rice from the bottom and sides of the pan. When the liquid has been almost completely absorbed, add another ½ cup (4 fl oz/125 ml) liquid, stirring continuously. Continue in this manner, stirring almost continuously and keeping the grains slightly moist at all times, until the rice is firm but tender and the kernels are no longer chalky at the center, 20–30 minutes. (If you run out of liquid before the rice is ready, add hot water.)

When the risotto is done, stir in another ½ cup (4 fl oz/125 ml) liquid, the squash, the toasted nuts and half of the Parmesan. Season to taste with salt and pepper. Transfer to a warmed serving dish and sprinkle with the remaining Parmesan. Serve at once. *Serves 6*

Luxurious lobster-nights, farewell,
For sober, studious days!

—Alexander Pope

Lobster with Tangerine-Chive Butter

For the tangerine-chive butter:

¾   **cup (6 oz/185 g) unsalted butter**

½   **teaspoon finely grated tangerine zest**

3   **tablespoons fresh tangerine juice**

1   **tablespoon Dijon mustard**

¼   **cup (⅓ oz/10 g) finely snipped fresh chives**

     salt and freshly ground pepper

For the lobsters:

4   **qt (4 l) water**

1   **tablespoon salt**

6   **live lobsters, 1¼–1½ lb (625–750 g) each**

Lobsters are the most prized members of the crustacean family, with the preferred variety being the Maine or American lobster. The meat comes primarily from the large, heavy front pincer claws and the tail. Spiny lobsters or rock lobsters swim in the warmer waters off the coast of Southern California, Mexico and Florida. Their meat is stringier and not nearly as sweet as that of Maine lobsters. For the best flavor and texture, look for lobsters with lots of life and cook them the same day they are purchased.

TO MAKE THE TANGERINE-CHIVE BUTTER, in a small saucepan, combine the butter, tangerine zest, tangerine juice, mustard and chives. Season to taste with salt and pepper. Place over medium heat and, as soon as the butter melts, remove from the heat. Let stand at room temperature for 1 hour.

To prepare the lobsters, 10–15 minutes before serving, bring the water to a boil in a large stockpot. Once it boils, add the salt and the lobsters, immersing them completely. Boil until dark red and fully cooked, about 10 minutes. Using tongs, transfer to a plate and let cool slightly.

Reheat the butter until warm and divide among 6 small sauce bowls. Serve 1 lobster per person accompanied with a small bowl of the warm butter.

To make eating the lobsters easier, crack the claws and cut down the underside of the tail with kitchen scissors, then serve the lobster with small forks or lobster picks for extracting the meat. *Serves 6*

The black turkey gobbler, the tips of his beautiful tail;
above us the dawn becomes yellow.

—Anonymous

Turkey with Chestnut Stuffing

1   turkey, 10–12 lb (5–6 kg), with the giblets

2   teaspoons salt, plus salt to taste

3   large yellow onions

6   cups (48 fl oz/1.5 l) chicken stock

1   carrot, peeled and coarsely chopped

6   fresh parsley stems

¼   teaspoon dried thyme

1   bay leaf

1½ lb (750 g) fresh chestnuts

¾   cup (6 oz/185 g) unsalted butter

¼   lb (125 g) lean bacon, diced

4   celery stalks, finely diced

¼   cup (⅓ oz/10 g) chopped fresh parsley

1   tablespoon chopped fresh thyme

1   tablespoon chopped fresh sage

11   cups (22 oz/685 g) cubed (½-inch/12-mm) firm-textured sourdough bread, left at room temperature for 2–3 days

     freshly ground pepper

1   tablespoon all-purpose (plain) flour

1   teaspoon cornstarch (corn-flour)

RINSE THE TURKEY and rub inside and out with the 2 teaspoons salt. Coarsely chop 1 onion and place in a saucepan. Finely dice the remaining 2 onions; set aside. Add the stock, carrot, parsley stems, dried thyme, bay leaf and giblets to the pan. Bring to a gentle simmer and cook, uncovered, for 1½ hours. Strain through a sieve. You should have about 5 cups (40 fl oz/1.25 l) stock.

Meanwhile, make a cut across the flat side of each chestnut. Place in a saucepan, add water to cover, bring to a simmer and cook until easily pierced, 45–55 minutes. Remove from the heat. Peel away the hard shells and inner sheaths while the chestnuts are still hot. Chop coarsely and place in a large bowl.

Preheat an oven to 400°F (200°C). In a frying pan over medium heat, melt ½ cup (4 oz/125 g) of the butter. Add the bacon, diced onions and celery and cook uncovered, stirring occasionally, until soft, about 12 minutes. Add to the chestnuts along with the chopped parsley, thyme and sage and the bread cubes. Toss and add enough stock (1–2 cups/8–16 fl oz/250–500 ml) for the mixture to form a ball when squeezed. Season with salt and pepper.

Stuff the body and neck cavities loosely with the stuffing and truss as directed on page 15. Place, breast side up, on an oiled rack in a roasting pan. Melt the remaining ¼ cup (2 oz/60 g) butter and brush 1 tablespoon on the turkey. Soak a large, double-layer piece of cheesecloth (muslin) in the remaining butter.

Roast for 45 minutes. Reduce the heat to 325°F (165°C). Drape the cheesecloth over the turkey and continue to roast, basting with pan drippings every 30 minutes, until the juices run clear when a thigh is pierced or an instant-read thermometer inserted into the thigh registers 180°F (82°C), 1½–2 hours longer. Transfer to a platter, cover loosely with foil and let stand for 20 minutes.

Reserve 2 tablespoons drippings in the pan (discard the rest) and place over high heat. Whisk together the flour, cornstarch and ½ cup (4 fl oz/125 ml) stock, then whisk into the pan. Add the remaining stock and stir until thickened, 2–3 minutes. Strain through a sieve into a sauceboat. Remove the cheesecloth, carve the turkey and serve with the stuffing and gravy. *Serves 6*

1   **roasting chicken, 3½–4 lb
(1.75–2 kg), giblets removed**

      **salt to taste, plus ¼ teaspoon
salt**

      **freshly ground pepper to
taste, plus ⅛ teaspoon ground
pepper**

1   **tablespoon chopped fresh sage**

1   **teaspoon chopped fresh
thyme**

½   **teaspoon chopped fresh
oregano**

½   **teaspoon chopped fresh
rosemary**

4   **thin lemon slices, seeds
removed**

2   **tablespoons unsalted butter,
melted**

Herb-Roasted Chicken

Robust herbs such as sage, thyme, oregano and rosemary produce tough leaves that stand up to cooler temperatures. In mild climates, these herbs flourish in gardens throughout the colder months, while in cold climates they can be grown indoors. Slipped under the skin of a whole roasting chicken, they add hearty flavor to one of the season's most venerable dishes.

PREHEAT AN OVEN to 375°F (190°C).

Rinse the chicken under cold water, drain and pat dry with paper towels. Season inside and outside with salt and pepper.

In a small bowl, mix together the sage, thyme, oregano, rosemary, ¼ teaspoon salt and ⅛ teaspoon pepper. Using your fingers, loosen the skin of the chicken that covers the breast by sliding your fingers between the skin and the flesh, being careful not to tear the skin. Slip half of the herbs inside the pocket defined by each breast half, distributing them evenly over the breast and thigh. Tuck the lemon slices inside the pockets between the skin and flesh, placing 2 slices on each side. Truss the chicken by tying the legs together with kitchen string. Brush the chicken with the melted butter.

Place the chicken on its side on an oiled roasting rack in a roasting pan. Roast the chicken for 20 minutes. Turn the chicken onto its other side and roast for another 20 minutes. Turn the chicken, breast side up, and continue to roast until an instant-read thermometer inserted into the thickest part of the breast away from the bone registers 160°F (71°C) and in the thigh registers 170°F (77°C), or until the juices run clear when the thigh is pierced with a knife, 15–20 minutes longer.

Remove the chicken from the oven and transfer to a platter. Cover loosely with aluminum foil and let stand for 10 minutes before carving.

To serve, carve the chicken and serve at once. *Serves 4*

Ham, Potato and Cheddar Cheese Gratin

2   cups (16 fl oz/500 ml) water

1   ham steak, 1½ lb (750 g) and ¼ inch (6 mm) thick, trimmed of all fat and cut into 1–1½-inch (2.5–4-cm) squares

3½   lb (1.75 kg) baking potatoes, peeled and cut into thin slices

3   cups (24 fl oz/750 ml) milk

¼   cup (2 oz/60 g) unsalted butter

6   tablespoons (2 oz/60 g) all-purpose (plain) flour

½   lb (250 g) extra-sharp Cheddar cheese, shredded

½   lb (250 g) smoked Cheddar cheese, shredded

2   tablespoons Dijon mustard

⅛   teaspoon cayenne pepper

     salt and freshly ground black pepper

The French term *gratin* means "crust," referring to the golden topping that develops when a dish such as this one is cooked in a large, shallow baking dish. The delectable results make a perfect buffet main course, surrounded with salads and assorted breads and rolls.

IN A SAUCEPAN over high heat, bring the water to a boil. Add the ham and simmer for 30 seconds. Remove from the heat and drain well. Set aside.

Oil a 9-by-13-inch (23-by-33-cm) baking dish. Distribute one-fourth of the potatoes evenly over the bottom of the prepared dish. Distribute one-third of the ham evenly over the potatoes. Top with half of the remaining potatoes and then all of the remaining ham. Top with all the remaining potatoes, layering the slices attractively.

Preheat an oven to 350°F (180°C).

Pour the milk into a saucepan placed over medium heat and warm until small bubbles appear at the edges of the pan. Remove from the heat.

In another saucepan over medium heat, melt the butter. Stir in the flour and cook, stirring constantly, for 2 minutes. (Do not brown.) Gradually stir in the hot milk and cook, stirring, until the mixture thickens, 4–5 minutes. Remove from the heat. Stir in the extra-sharp Cheddar cheese, smoked Cheddar cheese, mustard and cayenne pepper. Season to taste with salt and black pepper. Return the pan to low heat and stir just until the cheese melts, 1–2 minutes.

Pour the cheese sauce evenly over the potatoes and ham. Bake, uncovered, until the potatoes can be easily pierced with a skewer and the top is golden brown, about 1 hour.

To serve, spoon the gratin onto warmed individual plates and serve at once. *Serves 6–8*

Veal Scallopini with Orange and Fennel

1¼ lb (625 g) thin veal scallops, cut from the sirloin

5 tablespoons (2½ fl oz/75 ml) extra-virgin olive oil

½ teaspoon finely grated orange zest

¼ cup (2 fl oz/60 ml) fresh orange juice

1½ tablespoons balsamic vinegar

salt and freshly ground pepper

2 large seedless oranges

2 fennel bulbs

¾ cup (4 oz/125 g) all-purpose (plain) flour

2 eggs

2 cups (8 oz/250 g) fine dried bread crumbs

2 tablespoons water

3 tablespoons unsalted butter

¼ cup (⅓ oz/10 g) loosely packed fresh flat-leaf (Italian) parsley leaves

Fennel and orange form a delicious taste combination. For an elegant meal, accompany the veal with orange-scented rice and wilted kale.

PLACE EACH VEAL SCALLOP between 2 pieces of waxed paper and pound with a flat meat pounder to a thickness of about ¼ inch (6 mm). Set aside.

In a small bowl, whisk together 2 tablespoons of the oil, the orange zest and juice, vinegar, and salt and pepper to taste to form a vinaigrette. Set aside.

Using a sharp knife, cut a thick slice off the top and bottom of each orange to reveal the flesh. Then, standing each orange upright on a cutting surface, cut off the peel and white membrane in thick, wide strips. Working with 1 orange at a time, hold the orange over a bowl and cut along either side of each segment to free it from the membrane, letting the segments drop into the bowl. Set aside.

Trim off any stems and bruised outer stalks from the fennel bulbs. Cut the bulbs in half lengthwise, then cut crosswise into paper-thin slices. Set aside.

Place the flour, eggs and bread crumbs in 3 separate shallow bowls. Whisk the eggs lightly to blend them, then whisk in the water. Season the bread crumbs to taste with salt and pepper. Dredge both sides of each veal scallop with flour, shaking off the excess. Then, coat the veal scallops with the egg, letting the excess drip off. Finally, lightly coat both sides with bread crumbs.

In a large sauté pan over medium-high heat, melt 1½ tablespoons of the butter with 1½ tablespoons of the remaining olive oil. When hot, add half of the veal in a single layer. Sauté, turning occasionally, until golden brown on both sides, 3–4 minutes total. Repeat with the remaining butter, oil and veal.

To serve, divide evenly among 6 warmed individual plates. In a bowl, toss together the fennel, parsley, orange segments and vinaigrette. Top each serving of veal with some of the salad and serve at once. *Serves 6–8*

Pappardelle with Red Wine-Stewed Duck

1   tablespoon olive oil

1   duck, about 5 lb (2.5 kg), cut into 8 pieces and skin and excess fat removed

1   large yellow onion, diced

1   large celery stalk, diced

1   large carrot, peeled and diced

3   oz (90 g) pancetta, finely diced

3   cups (18 oz/560 g) peeled, seeded and chopped tomatoes (fresh or canned)

2½   cups (20 fl oz/625 ml) dry red wine such as Chianti, Barolo or Cabernet Sauvignon

1   tablespoon chopped fresh rosemary

    salt and freshly ground pepper

¾   lb (375 g) dried or fresh pappardelle noodles

½   cup (2 oz/60 g) freshly grated Parmesan cheese

Wild ducks are in season during the winter months when the birds fly south to feed. Use either a wild or pen-raised duck for this classic Tuscan preparation, which also works well with chicken, game hens or even rabbit. A crusty sourdough baguette, a tossed green salad and a full-bodied red wine are the ideal accompaniments.

IN A LARGE, HEAVY POT over medium-high heat, warm the olive oil. Add the duck pieces and cook, turning as needed, until they begin to turn golden, about 10 minutes. Add the onion, celery, carrot and pancetta and continue to cook until the onion is soft, about 10 minutes longer. Add the tomatoes, 1½ cups (12 fl oz/375 ml) of the red wine and the rosemary and bring to a boil. Reduce the heat to low, cover and simmer for 1 hour. Add the remaining 1 cup (8 fl oz/250 ml) red wine, stir well and continue to simmer, uncovered, until the meat begins to fall off the bones and the sauce has thickened slightly, about 1¼ hours longer.

Using tongs, transfer the duck pieces to a bowl and let stand until cool enough to handle. Remove the meat from the bones and tear into bite-sized pieces; discard the bones. Return the meat to the sauce and bring to a boil over medium heat. Simmer until the sauce thickens a bit more, 5–10 minutes. Season to taste with salt and pepper.

Meanwhile, bring a large pot three-fourths full of salted water to a rolling boil. Add the pappardelle, stir well and cook until al dente (firm but tender to the bite), 5–8 minutes. Drain the pappardelle and transfer to a large warmed serving bowl. Pour the sauce over the pasta and toss gently to coat evenly. Serve at once. Pass the Parmesan cheese at the table. *Serves 6*

Cracked Crab with Horseradish Mayonnaise

For the horseradish mayonnaise:

1   **egg yolk**

1   **teaspoon whole-grain mustard**

½   **cup (4 fl oz/125 ml) olive oil**

½   **cup (4 fl oz/125 ml) vegetable, corn or safflower oil**

2   **cloves garlic, minced**

1½   **tablespoons fresh lemon juice, or as needed**

3   **tablespoons prepared horseradish**

     salt and freshly ground pepper

2   **tablespoons warm water**

For the crabs:

4   **qt (4 l) water**

1   **tablespoon salt**

3   **live Dungeness crabs, 2–2½ lb (1–1.25 kg) each**

Cracked crab makes a simple, yet elegant main course for the holidays. Blue or stone crabs can be used if Dungeness are unavailable; adjust the cooking time accordingly. If time is short, purchase freshly cooked crabs and ask your fishmonger to do the cleaning and cracking.

TO MAKE THE HORSERADISH MAYONNAISE, in a small bowl, whisk together the egg yolk, mustard and 1 tablespoon of the olive oil until an emulsion forms. Combine the remaining olive oil and vegetable oil in a cup with a spout. Drop by drop at first and whisking constantly, gradually add the oil mixture to the emulsion. Stir in the garlic, 1½ tablespoons lemon juice and the horseradish. Season to taste with salt and pepper and more lemon juice, if needed. Whisking constantly, add the warm water to thin the mayonnaise slightly. Cover and refrigerate until needed.

To prepare the crabs, in a large pot, bring the water to a boil over high heat. Once it boils, add the salt and the crabs, immersing them completely. Boil until cooked and the shells are red, about 12 minutes. Using tongs, transfer the crabs to a plate and let cool slightly.

Working with 1 crab at a time, place the crab on its back. Pull off the small triangular apron-shaped shell flap and discard. Turn the crab over and lift up and snap off the large top shell and discard. Remove the dark gray intestines and the feather-shaped white spongy gills from the body and discard. Rinse the body well. Using a large, heavy knife, cut the body in half from the head to tail. Cut each half crosswise into thirds. Using a lobster cracker or a mallet, crack the claws and legs. If the crabs have cooled, warm them on a steamer rack over boiling water for 5–7 minutes.

To serve, arrange the crabs on a platter and serve with small forks or lobster picks for extracting the meat. Offer the horseradish mayonnaise on the side.
Serves 6

Cassoulet

2¼	cups (1 lb/500 g) dried Great Northern or flageolet beans
1	yellow onion pierced with 10 whole cloves
¾	lb (375 g) thickly sliced bacon, finely diced
2	lb (1 kg) boneless lamb cut from the leg, in one piece
2	lb (1 kg) pork loin, in one piece
	salt to taste, plus 1 teaspoon salt
	freshly ground pepper to taste, plus ½ teaspoon pepper
1	lb (500 g) Toulouse or other pork-and-garlic sausages
8	cloves garlic, minced
8	fresh parsley stems
1	teaspoon chopped fresh thyme
2	bay leaves
3	tablespoons tomato paste
1	teaspoon ground allspice
1½	cups (6 oz/185 g) fine dried bread crumbs

This abbreviated rendition of a classic peasant dish of southwestern France saves hours in the kitchen yet delivers authentic flavors.

PICK OVER THE BEANS and discard any damaged ones. Rinse, place in a bowl and add water to cover generously. Let soak for 3 hours. Drain and place in a saucepan with the onion and water to cover by 2 inches (5 cm). Bring to a boil, reduce the heat to low and simmer gently, uncovered, until almost tender, 40–50 minutes. Drain, discarding the onion and reserving the liquid.

Preheat an oven to 350°F (180°C). In a large ovenproof stew pot over low heat, fry the bacon until it begins to turn golden, about 5 minutes. Using a slotted spoon, transfer to a plate. Reserve the drippings in the pot.

Season the lamb and pork with salt and pepper and add to the stew pot. Place in the oven and roast, basting occasionally with the bacon drippings, until the meat is tender, about 1¼ hours. Remove from the oven, let cool and cut into 1-inch (2.5-cm) cubes. Set aside. Do not wash the pot.

Meanwhile, prick the sausages with a fork. Place in a frying pan, add water to cover halfway and simmer gently, turning once, until almost cooked through, about 12 minutes total. Drain, let cool and slice on the diagonal.

Place one-third of the drained beans in the reserved pot. Sprinkle with half of the bacon, lamb, pork, sausage, garlic and salt and pepper to taste. Using kitchen string, tie the parsley, thyme and bay leaves into a bundle. Add to the pot. Repeat the layers, using half of the remaining beans and all of the remaining garlic, meats and sausage. Season to taste with salt and pepper and top with the remaining beans.

In a bowl, whisk together the tomato paste, allspice, the 1 teaspoon salt, the ½ teaspoon pepper and 2 cups (16 fl oz/500 ml) of the reserved bean liquid. Pour into the pot just to cover the beans. Bake, uncovered, for 1 hour; add more bean liquid, if necessary, to prevent the beans from drying out. Sprinkle with the bread crumbs and continue to bake until golden, about 1 hour longer.

Discard the herb bundle and serve directly from the pot. *Serves 8–10*

Crown Roast of Pork with Baked Apples

1   **crown roast of pork with 16 chops, 6 lb (3 kg)**

     salt and freshly ground pepper

8   **apples** *(see note)*

½   **cup (4 fl oz/125 ml) late-harvest white wine or French Sauterne**

¼   **cup (3 oz/90 g) honey**

3   **tablespoons unsalted butter**

½   **teaspoon finely grated lemon zest**

½   **teaspoon ground cinnamon**

¼   **teaspoon ground cloves**

A crown roast is formed by joining two center racks of rib chops into a circle, their rib ends trimmed to resemble the points of a crown. Although it isn't too difficult to form the roast yourself, most good butchers will do it for you. Winter baking apples such as McIntosh, Cortland or Granny Smith complement the meat's inherent sweetness, as do wines like Gewürztraminer or Riesling.

PREHEAT AN OVEN to 400°F (200°C).

Place a rack in a shallow roasting pan and set the crown roast on it. Season to taste with salt and pepper. Roast uncovered for 30 minutes. Reduce the heat to 325°F (165°C) and continue to roast, basting frequently with the pan juices, until an instant-read thermometer inserted into the center of the loin away from the bone registers 150°F (65°C), or until the meat is pale pink when cut in the thickest part, about 1 hour and 15 minutes longer; check the pork periodically and cover the rib bone ends with foil if they begin to burn before the meat is done.

While the pork is roasting, peel the top third of each apple and then core the apples. In a small saucepan over high heat, combine the wine, honey, butter, lemon zest, cinnamon and cloves and bring to a boil. Remove from the heat and set aside.

About 15 minutes before the pork is done, place the apples in a 2-qt (2-l) baking dish and pour the honey mixture evenly over them. Cover with aluminum foil and place in the oven with the pork. Cook the apples until tender when pierced with a knife, 20–25 minutes, checking periodically during baking to prevent drying. When the pork is done, remove it from the oven and cover loosely with aluminum foil. Let stand for 10 minutes before carving.

Place the roast on a warmed platter and arrange the baked apples alongside. Drizzle the juices from the baking dish over the apples and the pork. At the table, cut the roast between the rib bones and serve with the apples. *Serves 8*

salads and side dishes

Annihilating all that's made
To a green thought in a green shade.

—Andrew Marvell

Romaine and Escarole Salad with Warm Duck Livers

For the vinaigrette:

5 tablespoons (2½ fl oz/75 ml) extra-virgin olive oil

1 clove garlic, minced

1½ tablespoons whole-grain mustard

3 tablespoons red wine vinegar

salt and freshly ground pepper

For the salad:

1 head escarole (Batavian endive), tough stems removed and leaves torn into large pieces

1 head romaine lettuce, tough stems removed and leaves cut crosswise into strips 1 inch (2.5 cm) wide

For the croutons:

¼ lb (125 g) country-style bread, crusts removed

3 tablespoons unsalted butter

2 cloves garlic, minced

salt and freshly ground pepper

For the livers:

¾ lb (375 g) duck livers

1 tablespoon unsalted butter

The crucial step to preparing this delicious winter salad is to cook the livers so that they are still pink in the center. Overcooking them yields a leathery texture and strong flavor. This salad can also be made with chicken livers, for which the same cooking precautions apply.

PREHEAT AN OVEN to 400°F (200°C).

To make the vinaigrette, in a small bowl, whisk together the olive oil, garlic, mustard, vinegar and salt and pepper to taste. Set aside.

Place the escarole and romaine lettuce in a large bowl.

To make the croutons, tear the bread into ½-inch (12-mm) pieces or cut into 1-inch (2.5-cm) cubes and spread on a baking sheet. Combine the butter and garlic in a small saucepan and place over medium heat. When the butter has melted, pour it evenly over the bread, season to taste with salt and pepper and toss well. Bake, stirring once or twice, until golden and crisp, 10–15 minutes. Remove from the oven and let cool. (Store in an airtight container at room temperature if not using immediately. The croutons will keep for up to 4 days.)

To prepare the livers, trim away any membranes. In a large frying pan over medium heat, melt the butter. Add the livers in a single layer and cook, turning occasionally, until slightly firm to the touch but still pink inside, 2–3 minutes. Season to taste with salt and pepper.

Remove the livers from the heat and immediately transfer to the bowl containing the escarole and romaine lettuce. Drizzle with the vinaigrette and toss gently. Place the salad on a large platter. Sprinkle the croutons over the top and serve at once. *Serves 6*

Beet Salad with Stilton and Walnuts

⅓   cup (1½ oz/45 g) walnut halves

2   lb (1 kg) red or yellow beets

2   tablespoons olive oil

    salt and freshly ground pepper

3½   tablespoons extra-virgin olive oil

2½   tablespoons red wine vinegar

1½   cups (2 oz/60 g) loosely packed watercress, tough stems removed

3   oz (90 g) Stilton cheese, crumbled

Blessed with the lovely color of deep garnet or golden orange, beets are firm, round, hardy root vegetables. It is best to bake them rather than boil them, as baking intensifies their sweetness.

PREHEAT AN OVEN to 375°F (190°C). Spread the walnut halves on a baking sheet and toast until lightly browned and fragrant, 5–7 minutes. Remove from the oven and let cool. Leave the oven set at 375°F (190°C).

Rinse each beet with cold water and trim away all but ½ inch (12 mm) of the stem. Put the beets in a shallow baking dish and drizzle with the olive oil. Roll the beets to coat them with the oil and season to taste with salt and pepper. Cover with aluminum foil.

Bake until the beets are tender when pierced with a knife, 50–60 minutes. Remove from the oven and set aside until cool enough to handle. Slip off the skins and cut each beet into thin wedges. Place in a bowl.

Meanwhile, in a small bowl, whisk together the extra-virgin olive oil, vinegar and salt and pepper to taste to form a vinaigrette. Drizzle three-fourths of the vinaigrette over the beets, toss well and let cool completely.

Place the watercress in a serving bowl, drizzle with the remaining vinaigrette and toss to coat. Add the beets and toss again to coat. Season to taste with salt and pepper. Distribute the crumbled Stilton and the walnuts evenly over the top and serve. *Serves 6*

A seed hidden in the heart of an apple is an orchard invisible.

—Welsh Proverb

½   **cup (2 oz/60 g) walnut pieces**

1½   **tablespoons white wine vinegar**

¼   **cup (2 fl oz/60 ml) extra-virgin olive oil**

     salt and freshly ground pepper

1   **small head escarole (Batavian endive), tough stems removed and leaves torn into 1½-inch (4-cm) pieces**

2   **heads Belgian endive (chicory/witloof), trimmed and cut lengthwise into thin strips**

2   **celery stalks, cut on the sharp diagonal into thin slices**

1   **Granny Smith, pippin or other tart green apple, halved, cored and thinly sliced lengthwise**

     shaved Parmesan cheese

Winter White Salad with Apples and Parmesan

The pale hues of some of this season's fresh ingredients are no indication of the wonderfully vibrant flavors they can impart to a salad bowl. For a touch of color, add a small head of radicchio, cut into thin strips. Pears may be substituted for the apples and pecans for the walnuts.

PREHEAT AN OVEN to 375°F (190°C). Spread the walnuts on a baking sheet and toast until lightly browned and fragrant, 5–7 minutes. Remove from the oven and let cool.

In a small bowl, whisk together the vinegar, olive oil and salt and pepper to taste to form a vinaigrette.

In a large salad bowl, toss together the escarole, endive and celery. Add the apple and walnuts, drizzle with the vinaigrette and toss well. Garnish with shaved Parmesan and serve immediately. *Serves 6*

Citrus Salad with Mint and Red Onions

3	**large, seedless oranges**
2	**blood oranges**
1	**Ruby grapefruit or other pink grapefruit**
¼	**small red (Spanish) onion, very thinly sliced**
3	**tablespoons fresh orange juice**
1	**tablespoon red wine vinegar**
3	**tablespoons extra-virgin olive oil**
	salt and freshly ground pepper
2	**tablespoons coarsely chopped fresh mint**
6	**kumquats, thinly sliced and seeds discarded**
	seeds from ¼ pomegranate

Citrus fruits are at their best during the winter months when they grow in profusion in tropical and temperate climates. Use any sweet citrus fruits for this recipe, such as oranges, blood oranges, tangerines, tangelos, mandarin oranges, grapefruits, pomelos and even kumquats.

HOLDING 1 ORANGE over a small bowl, finely grate enough zest to measure 1 teaspoon. Using a sharp knife, cut a thick slice off the tops and bottoms of the oranges, blood oranges and grapefruit to reveal the flesh. Working with 1 fruit at a time, place it upright on a cutting surface and cut off the peel and white membrane in wide strips. Cut the oranges and grapefruit crosswise into slices ¼ inch (6 mm) thick. Cut the grapefruit slices into quarters. Using the tip of the knife, remove any seeds and discard. Arrange the orange and grapefruit slices on a serving platter, overlapping the various colors. Separate the onion slices and scatter over the top.

Add the orange juice, vinegar and olive oil to the bowl containing the orange zest. Season to taste with salt and pepper and whisk to form a vinaigrette. Drizzle the vinaigrette evenly over the citrus and onion. Sprinkle with the mint, kumquat slices and pomegranate seeds. Serve immediately. *Serves 6*

Grilled Scallop, Pink Grapefruit and Frisée Salad

1   **large pink grapefruit**

1   **tablespoon balsamic vinegar**

2   **tablespoons fresh grapefruit juice**

¼   **cup (2 fl oz/60 ml) extra-virgin olive oil**

     salt and freshly ground pepper

1   **lb (500 g) sea scallops, cut in half horizontally**

1   **tablespoon olive oil**

1   **head frisée, tough stems removed, torn into small pieces**

Large sea scallops are at their best from mid-autumn to early spring, making this salad with cold-weather citrus and greens an ideal light entrée for a winter meal. You could, if you wish, substitute smaller bay scallops, which reach their peak in late autumn. Buy scallops that look plump and moist and have a fresh, clean scent of the sea.

HOLDING THE GRAPEFRUIT over a small bowl, finely grate enough zest to measure 1 teaspoon. Using a sharp knife, cut a thick slice off the top and bottom of the grapefruit to reveal the flesh. Then, standing the grapefruit upright on a cutting surface, cut off the peel and white membrane in thick, wide strips. Cut the grapefruit crosswise into slices ¼ inch (6 mm) thick. Using the tip of the knife, remove any seeds and discard. Cut each slice into quarters and place in a large bowl. Set aside.

To the bowl containing the grapefruit zest, add the balsamic vinegar, grapefruit juice and the extra-virgin olive oil. Season to taste with salt and pepper and whisk to form a vinaigrette.

Preheat a ridged cast-iron grill pan or frying pan over medium heat. Brush the scallops with the olive oil. When the pan is hot, add the scallops in a single layer. Cook until seared on one side, about 1 minute. Turn over the scallops, season to taste with salt and pepper and continue to cook until seared on the second side and just firm to the touch, about 1 minute longer. Remove from the pan.

Add the scallops and the frisée to the bowl containing the grapefruit. Drizzle with the vinaigrette, season to taste with salt and pepper and toss well.

Transfer the salad to a platter or individual plates and serve at once. *Serves 6*

Wild Rice Pilaf with Dried Fruits and Pecans

½   **cup (2 oz/60 g) pecans**

1½   **cups (9 oz/280 g) wild rice**

3   **tablespoons unsalted butter**

1   **small yellow onion, minced**

2¼   **cups (18 fl oz/560 ml) water**

2¼   **cups (18 fl oz/560 ml) chicken stock**

¾   **teaspoon salt**

¼   **teaspoon ground cinnamon**

¼   **teaspoon ground allspice**

⅛   **teaspoon freshly grated nutmeg**

⅛   **teaspoon freshly ground pepper, plus pepper to taste**

½   **cup (3 oz/90 g) dried apricot halves, coarsely chopped**

¼   **cup (1½ oz/45 g) golden raisins (sultanas)**

¼   **cup (1 oz/30 g) dried cranberries**

¼   **cup (1 oz/30 g) dried pitted cherries**

Wild rice is actually not a rice at all, but the seeds of a long-grain marsh grass native to the northern Great Lakes region of the United States. It is now cultivated in California and several Midwest states as well. Dried apples can be added in place of the apricots along with the other dried fruits, and almonds, pine nuts, walnuts, cashews or pistachios can be substituted for the pecans.

PREHEAT AN OVEN to 375°F (190°C). Spread the pecans on a baking sheet and toast until lightly browned and fragrant, 5–7 minutes. Remove from the oven, let cool and chop coarsely. Set aside.

Meanwhile, place the rice in a bowl and add water to cover. Stir the rice to rinse it, then drain well and set aside. In a saucepan over medium heat, melt the butter. Add the onion and sauté, stirring occasionally, until soft, about 10 minutes. Add the wild rice, water, stock, salt, cinnamon, allspice, nutmeg and ⅛ teaspoon pepper. Bring to a boil, reduce the heat to low, cover and simmer gently, without stirring, until the rice is almost tender and most of the liquid has been absorbed, 40–45 minutes.

Add the apricots, raisins, cranberries and cherries. Stir to combine, re-cover and continue to cook until the rice is tender and all the liquid has been absorbed, 5–10 minutes longer. If the wild rice is still not tender at this point and liquid remains, re-cover and cook for a few minutes longer.

Add the pecans and toss to mix well. Season to taste with pepper. Transfer to a warmed bowl and serve at once. *Serves 6*

Wilted Kale with Lemon and Garlic

2   tablespoons extra-virgin olive oil

2   tablespoons fresh lemon juice

2   cloves garlic, minced

    salt and freshly ground pepper

2   teaspoons olive oil

2   bunches kale, about 2 lb (1 kg) total weight, stems removed and carefully rinsed

The robust flavor of kale offers the perfect canvas for pairing with other, equally intense flavors. Loaded with vitamins A and C, kale provides a healthy and hearty alternative to spinach and Swiss chard (silverbeet). It grows well in cold climates and, although available year-round, is best during the winter months. Garnish with lemon zest, if desired.

IN A SMALL BOWL, whisk together the extra-virgin olive oil, lemon juice, garlic and salt and pepper to taste to form a vinaigrette. Set aside.

In a large frying pan over medium heat, warm the olive oil. Cut the kale crosswise into 1-inch (2.5-cm) strips and add to the pan. Cover and cook, stirring occasionally, until the kale wilts, 5–7 minutes. Uncover, drizzle the vinaigrette over the kale and toss well. Season to taste with salt and pepper.

Place on a warmed platter and serve at once. *Serves 6*

O my garden gleaming cold and white,
Thou hast outshone the far faint moon on high.

—Yüan Mee

Purée of White Winter Vegetables

4	baking potatoes, peeled and coarsely chopped
2	turnips, peeled and coarsely chopped
1	large yellow onion, peeled and quartered
1	celery root (celeriac), 1½ lb (750 g), peeled and coarsely chopped
10	cloves garlic
2	tablespoons unsalted butter
2	tablespoons heavy (double) cream
3	tablespoons white wine vinegar
	salt and freshly ground pepper

Common potatoes and turnips combine with the lesser-known celery root in this delicious purée. Celery root has an earthy flavor not unlike a cross between stalk celery and parsley. A type of celery cultivated specifically for the root, it is often eaten raw in salads or cooked in soups and stews.

PLACE THE POTATOES, turnips, onion, celery root and garlic in a saucepan. Add water to cover and bring to a boil. Reduce the heat to low and simmer, uncovered, until the vegetables are completely tender when pierced with a knife, 20–25 minutes. Drain well, pressing the vegetables with the back of a spoon to drain off all the liquid.

In a small saucepan over medium heat, melt the butter. Stir in the cream and remove from the heat. Place the drained vegetables in a food processor fitted with the metal blade and pulse several times until puréed.

Transfer the mixture to a clean saucepan. Stir in the butter-cream mixture and the vinegar. Place over medium heat and reheat to serving temperature. Season to taste with salt and pepper. Spoon the purée into a serving dish and serve hot. *Serves 6*

Better is a dinner of herbs where love is,
than a stalled ox and hatred therewith.

—Proverb

Winter Herb and Lemon Spaetzle

2	cups (10 oz/315 g) all-purpose (plain) flour
3	tablespoons chopped fresh chives
2	tablespoons chopped fresh sage
2	tablespoons chopped fresh flat-leaf (Italian) parsley
1	tablespoon chopped fresh thyme
2	teaspoons chopped fresh winter savory, optional
1	teaspoon finely grated lemon zest
5	eggs
⅔	cup (5 fl oz/160 ml) milk
¾	teaspoon salt
⅛	teaspoon freshly ground pepper
1	tablespoon unsalted butter, melted

Spaetzle are tiny dumplings that originated in Germany and Austria. Served simply with melted butter, they are among that region's cherished comfort foods. Most spaetzle are formed by hand, although inexpensive spaetzle makers—typically a colanderlike tool for releasing the batter—can be found in cookware shops.

BUTTER A LARGE ceramic baking dish and set aside.

Place the flour, all the herbs and the lemon zest in a bowl. In another bowl, whisk together the eggs until blended. Gradually whisk the eggs into the flour mixture. Stir in the milk, salt and pepper. Let stand for 30 minutes.

Preheat an oven to 275°F (135°C).

Bring a large pot three-fourths full of water to a boil. Working in batches, pour some of the batter into a large colander and, using the back of a large spoon, push strips of batter into the water. Alternatively, force the batter through the holes of a spaetzle maker into the water. As soon as the dumplings float to the surface, after 1–2 minutes, they are cooked. Using a slotted spoon, transfer them to the prepared baking dish and place them in the oven to dry the excess moisture. As each batch of dumplings is cooked, add it to the baking dish, gently tossing the freshly cooked dumplings with those already in the dish.

To serve, drizzle with the melted butter and toss gently to coat. Serve hot.
Serves 6

Nature is often hidden; sometimes overcome;
seldom extinguished.

—Francis Bacon

Broccoli Rabe with Pancetta and Kalamata Olives

4	tablespoons (2 fl oz/60 ml) olive oil
½	cup (2 oz/60 g) coarsely ground dried bread crumbs
	salt and freshly ground pepper
¼	lb (125 g) pancetta, finely diced
3	bunches young, tender broccoli rabe, tough stems removed (about 2½ lb/ 1.25 kg trimmed)
3	tablespoons fresh lemon juice
3	cloves garlic, minced
½	cup (2½ oz/75 g) Kalamata olives, pitted and thinly sliced

Buy broccoli rabe, also known as rapini, rape and cima di broccoli, when it is young and tender. As the flowers and stems grow larger, they become more pungent and bitter. Look for this cabbage family member in late fall through spring.

IN A LARGE FRYING PAN over medium heat, warm 2 tablespoons of the olive oil. Add the bread crumbs and toss constantly until lightly golden, 1–3 minutes. Season to taste with salt and pepper. Transfer to a small bowl and set aside.

Pour the remaining 2 tablespoons olive oil into the frying pan and place over medium heat. Add the pancetta and cook, stirring often, until lightly golden and almost crisp, 3–4 minutes. Add the broccoli rabe and cook, stirring often, until it wilts completely but is still bright green, 6–8 minutes.

Raise the heat to high and add the lemon juice, garlic and olives. Continue to cook, stirring constantly, until well mixed, about 1 minute. Season to taste with salt and pepper.

Transfer to a warmed platter and sprinkle with the reserved bread crumbs. Serve immediately. *Serves 6*

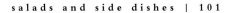

I have often thought that if heaven had given me choice of my position and calling, it should have been on a rich spot of earth, well watered, and near a good market for the productions of the garden.

—Thomas Jefferson

Pan-Roasted Winter Vegetables

½ lb (250 g) rutabagas (swedes), peeled and cut into pieces

½ lb (250 g) carrots, peeled and cut into pieces

½ lb (250 g) parsnips, peeled and cut into pieces

½ lb (250 g) Brussels sprouts, trimmed

½ lb (250 g) yams or sweet potatoes, peeled and cut into pieces

1 tablespoon unsalted butter

1 tablespoon extra-virgin olive oil

2 teaspoons chopped fresh thyme

2 teaspoons chopped fresh sage

⅛ teaspoon freshly grated nutmeg

salt and freshly ground pepper

½ cup (4 fl oz/125 ml) Marsala wine

This mélange of fresh vegetables combines members of the cabbage family—rutabagas and Brussels sprouts—with such roots and tubers as carrots, parsnips and yams or sweet potatoes. Although most roots and tubers are harvested in the autumn months, their long storage capability makes them favorite winter ingredients as well.

PREHEAT AN OVEN to 450°F (230°C).

Bring a large pot three-fourths full of salted water to a boil. Add the rutabagas, carrots and parsnips and simmer until the vegetables give slightly when pierced with a fork, about 4 minutes. Drain well.

Place the rutabagas, carrots, parsnips, Brussels sprouts, and yams or sweet potatoes in a large roasting pan. In a small saucepan over low heat, melt the butter. Add the olive oil, thyme, sage and nutmeg and stir to mix well. Drizzle the butter mixture over the vegetables and toss to coat evenly. Season to taste with salt and pepper. Pour the Marsala into the bottom of the roasting pan. Cover tightly with aluminum foil.

Bake for 40 minutes. Remove the foil, toss the vegetables and continue to bake, uncovered, until the Marsala evaporates and the vegetables can be easily pierced with a knife, 20–30 minutes.

Place the roasted vegetables on a warmed platter and serve at once. *Serves 6*

desserts

Polenta Custard with Port-Stewed Winter Fruits

For the stewed fruits:

3   cups (24 fl oz/750 ml) port wine

3   tablespoons honey

10 whole cloves

3   pears, preferably Bosc, peeled, halved and cored

1⅛ cups (7 oz/220 g) large dried apricots

For the polenta custard:

¼   cup (2 fl oz/60 ml) grappa or other brandy

¼   cup (1½ oz/45 g) golden raisins (sultanas)

2¼ cups (18 fl oz/560 ml) milk

⅛   teaspoon salt

¾   cup (4 oz/125 g) Italian polenta

1   cup (8 oz/250 g) ricotta cheese

½   cup (4 oz/125 g) sugar

¼   teaspoon ground cinnamon

3   eggs, lightly beaten

For the topping:

⅓   cup (3 fl oz/80 ml) crème fraîche blended with 2 tablespoons milk

    confectioners' (icing) sugar

TO MAKE THE STEWED FRUITS, in a saucepan over high heat, combine the port, honey and cloves. Bring to a boil, then reduce the heat to medium-low so that the port simmers. Add the pear halves and cook gently until tender and slightly translucent but not mushy, 20–30 minutes. Using a slotted spoon, transfer the pears to a cutting board. Discard the cloves. Add the apricots to the simmering port and cook gently until soft, about 10 minutes. Meanwhile, cut the pear halves lengthwise into wedges. When the apricots are done, remove the pan from the heat and add the pear wedges. Set aside.

To make the polenta custard, in a saucepan over medium heat, warm the brandy until hot. Remove from the heat, add the raisins and let stand for 30 minutes. In a large saucepan over high heat, combine the milk and salt. Bring to a boil, reduce the heat to medium and slowly whisk in the polenta. Continue to whisk for 2–3 minutes. Change to a wooden spoon and continue to simmer, stirring periodically, until the polenta is almost thick enough to hold the spoon upright, 15–20 minutes.

Preheat an oven to 375°F (190°C). Generously butter six ½-cup (4-fl oz/125-ml) ramekins.

In a large bowl, mix together the ricotta and sugar. Add the cooked polenta and stir well. Drain the raisins and add them with the cinnamon to the polenta. Stir in the eggs. Distribute evenly among the prepared ramekins. Place the ramekins, spaced well apart, on a baking sheet. Bake until set and a knife inserted into the center of a custard comes out clean, 20–22 minutes.

Just before the custards are done, gently reheat the fruits. Divide them and their liquid among 6 individual plates. Loosen the edges of the custards with a knife and invert them over the fruits. Drizzle with the crème fraîche mixture. Dust the tops with confectioners' sugar and serve. *Serves 6*

Persimmon Pudding

¾ cup (3 oz/90 g) coarsely chopped pecans

2 ripe Hachiya persimmons *(see note)*

1¾ cups (9 oz/280 g) all-purpose (plain) flour

2 teaspoons baking powder

½ teaspoon baking soda (bicarbonate of soda)

1 teaspoon ground cinnamon

½ teaspoon ground ginger

¼ teaspoon freshly grated nutmeg

1¼ cups (9 oz/280 g) firmly packed dark brown sugar

2 eggs

1 cup (8 fl oz/250 ml) milk

¾ cup (4½ oz/140 g) golden raisins (sultanas)

boiling water, as needed

⅓ cup (3 fl oz/80 ml) brandy

vanilla ice cream

Two of the most common persimmon varieties are the Hachiya and the Fuyu, both available from October to February. For this recipe you will want the larger Hachiya fruits, and will need to let them ripen until completely soft.

PREHEAT AN OVEN to 375°F (190°C). Generously butter a 2-qt (2-l) steamed pudding mold and its cover.

Spread the pecans on a baking sheet and toast until lightly browned and fragrant, 5–7 minutes. Remove from the oven and let cool. Reduce the oven temperature to 350°F (180°C).

Cut off the top from each persimmon, then cut in half. Scrape the pulp from the skin into a food processor fitted with the metal blade or into a blender. Purée until smooth; you should have 1 cup (8 fl oz/250 ml) purée.

Sift together the flour, baking powder, baking soda, cinnamon, ginger and nutmeg into a large bowl. In another bowl, combine the persimmon pulp, brown sugar, eggs and milk; whisk until blended. Gradually stir the persimmon mixture into the flour mixture until fully combined. Let the batter stand until thickened to the consistency of thin sour cream, about 20 minutes.

Stir the pecans and raisins into the batter. Pour into the prepared mold; cover with well-buttered waxed paper, overlapping the rim slightly, and then the cover. Place the mold in a larger baking pan in the oven. Pour boiling water into the baking pan to reach one-third up the sides of the mold. Bake until set and a skewer inserted into the center comes out clean, 2½–3 hours; check periodically and add water as needed to maintain its original level. Remove the mold from the baking pan and let stand, covered, for 10 minutes.

To serve, remove the cover, invert the pudding onto a serving plate and lift off the mold. In a small saucepan, warm the brandy over medium heat just until it begins to bubble around the edges. Immediately remove from the heat and ignite with a match. Pour the flaming brandy over the warm pudding. When the flames die, serve the pudding at once with ice cream. *Serves 8*

And still she slept an azure-lidded sleep,
In blanched linen, smooth, and lavender'd
While he from forth the closet brought a heap
Of candied apple, quince, and plum, and gourd.

—John Keats

Cinnamon-Poached Quinces with Nutmeg Cream

8	cups (64 fl oz/2 l) water
2	cups (1 lb/500 g) granulated sugar
5	cinnamon sticks
5	quinces, about 10 oz (315 g) each, peeled, halved, cored and cut into eighths
1	cup (8 fl oz/250 ml) heavy (double) cream
1	tablespoon confectioners' (icing) sugar
½	teaspoon freshly grated nutmeg

Sweet spices contribute a heartwarming quality to this homestyle dessert featuring a time-honored fruit of early winter. If you wish, you can cook the quinces up to 1 week in advance, allowing them to cool in their poaching liquid before storing them in the refrigerator. Reheat the fruit in their liquid before serving.

IN A LARGE SAUCEPAN over high heat, combine the water, granulated sugar and cinnamon sticks. Bring to a boil, stirring occasionally, and add the quinces. Reduce the heat to low and simmer, uncovered, until the quinces are tender and have turned a deep rose color, 2–2½ hours. Add water during cooking if necessary to keep the fruit covered with the poaching liquid. Do not stir the quinces while they are simmering; instead, move them about gently if necessary for even cooking.

Before serving, in a large bowl, using a whisk or an electric mixer, beat the cream until soft peaks form. Stir in the confectioners' sugar and the nutmeg. Cover and refrigerate until serving.

To serve, using a slotted spoon, transfer the warm quinces to a serving bowl. Serve the cream on the side. *Serves 6*

Nutmegs and ginger, cinnamon and cloves,
And they gave me this jolly red nose.

—Thomas Ravenscroft

Panforte

Panforte is a rich, intense and chewy Italian confection made from candied fruits, nuts and spices. In Tuscany, brightly wrapped packages of the dark, candylike cake are a telltale sign that Christmas is around the corner. If stored in an airtight container, the cake will keep at room temperature for at least a month. Serve in thin wedges with strong coffee.

PREHEAT AN OVEN to 375°F (190°C). Butter an 8-inch (20-cm) round cake pan and line the bottom with a piece of parchment paper cut to fit precisely.

Spread the almonds and hazelnuts on a baking sheet, keeping them separate, and toast until lightly browned and fragrant, 5–7 minutes. Remove from the oven, place the almonds on a cutting board and place the hazelnuts on a kitchen towel. Rub the hazelnuts with the towel to remove the skins. Do not worry if bits of skin remain. Place the hazelnuts on the board with the almonds. Coarsely chop all the nuts and place in a large bowl. Reduce the oven temperature to 350°F (180°C).

Add the candied peel, flour, cinnamon, cloves, coriander, nutmeg, allspice and pepper to the nuts and mix well.

In a small saucepan over medium heat, combine the honey and granulated sugar and heat, stirring occasionally, until the sugar melts, about 3 minutes. Stir the honey mixture into the almond-fruit mixture, mixing well. Transfer the batter to the prepared pan and, when cool enough to handle, wet your hands and press the mixture evenly into the pan.

Bake until golden brown, 30–35 minutes. Remove from the oven and invert onto a rack. Lift off the pan and let cool. When cool, peel off the parchment. Using a sifter or sieve, dust the top liberally with confectioners' sugar.

Makes one 8-inch (20-cm) cake; serves 8

¾ **cup (4 oz/125 g) almonds**

½ **cup (2½ oz/75 g) hazelnuts (filberts)**

1¼ **cups (7½ oz/235 g) mixed candied citrus peel, chopped**

⅓ **cup (2 oz/60 g) all-purpose (plain) flour**

1 **teaspoon ground cinnamon**

½ **teaspoon ground cloves**

½ **teaspoon ground coriander**

½ **teaspoon freshly grated nutmeg**

½ **teaspoon ground allspice**

⅛ **teaspoon ground white pepper**

½ **cup (6 oz/185 g) honey**

¼ **cup (2 oz/60 g) granulated sugar**

confectioners' (icing) sugar

1½	cups (7½ oz/235 g) all-purpose (plain) flour
1¼	teaspoons baking soda (bicarbonate of soda)
1½	teaspoons ground cinnamon
½	teaspoon ground ginger
¼	teaspoon ground cloves
¼	teaspoon freshly grated nutmeg
⅛	teaspoon salt
½	cup (4 oz/125 g) unsalted butter, at room temperature
⅔	cup (5 oz/155 g) sugar, plus about 5 tablespoons (2½ oz/75 g) sugar for dusting tops
½	teaspoon vanilla extract (essence)
1	egg yolk
¼	cup (3 oz/90 g) molasses

The Best Gingersnaps

Double or triple this recipe around the holidays and have several rolls of the icebox cookies on hand in the freezer to bake on the spur of the moment. They are irresistible served with espresso, tea or hot spiced cider, or packed into colorful tins for gift giving.

SIFT TOGETHER THE FLOUR, baking soda, cinnamon, ginger, cloves, nutmeg and salt into a bowl. In a large bowl, using an electric mixer set on high speed, cream together the butter and ⅔ cup (5 oz/155 g) sugar until light and fluffy, 1–2 minutes. Beat in the vanilla, egg yolk and molasses, mixing well. Add the flour mixture to the butter mixture in 3 batches, mixing on low speed until each addition is fully blended. Cover with plastic wrap and chill for 1 hour.

Place the chilled dough on a piece of plastic wrap and shape it into a rough log about 1½ inches (4 cm) in diameter. Wrap the log in the plastic wrap and roll it back and forth until the surface of the log is smooth and even. Refrigerate the roll for 2 hours or freeze for up to 2 months.

Preheat an oven to 375°F (190°C). Lightly oil 3 baking sheets.

Remove the roll from the refrigerator or freezer and unwrap it. Cut it into slices ⅛ inch (3 mm) thick and place them, 1 inch (2.5 cm) apart, on the baking sheets. Sprinkle the tops with ½ teaspoon sugar each.

If using 1 oven, place 2 baking sheets at a time in the oven; refrigerate the remaining sheet until ready to bake. Bake the cookies until golden around the edges but still soft, 8–10 minutes for chewy cookies and 10–12 minutes for crisp cookies; switch the pans halfway through the baking time. Using a spatula, immediately transfer the cookies to racks to cool. Store in an airtight container at room temperature for up to 3 days. *Makes about 2½ dozen cookies*

The proof of the pudding is in the eating.

—Miguel de Cervantes

Wintertime Bread Pudding

For the crème anglaise:

2 cups (16 fl oz/500 ml) milk

¼ cup (2 oz/60 g) granulated sugar

4 egg yolks

½ teaspoon vanilla extract

2 tablespoons dark rum

For the pudding:

½ cup (3 oz/90 g) dried apricots, halved

½ cup (2 oz/60 g) dried pitted cherries

1 cup (8 fl oz/250 ml) dark rum or brandy

6 tablespoons (3 oz/90 g) unsalted butter

3 Bosc pears, peeled, cored and thinly sliced lengthwise

10 slices coarse-textured white bread, crusts removed and halved on the diagonal

1 cup (8 fl oz/250 ml) milk

1 cup (8 fl oz/250 ml) heavy (double) cream

⅔ cup (5 oz/155 g) granulated sugar

½ teaspoon ground nutmeg

1 teaspoon vanilla extract

3 egg yolks, plus 3 whole eggs

boiling water, as needed

confectioners' (icing) sugar

TO MAKE THE CRÈME ANGLAISE, place the milk in a saucepan over medium heat. When bubbles appear at the pan edges, stir in the sugar until dissolved. Remove from the heat. In a bowl, whisk the egg yolks until blended. Gradually whisk in about ½ cup (4 fl oz/125 ml) of the hot milk. Then whisk the yolk-milk mixture into the milk remaining in the saucepan. Return to medium heat and cook, stirring, until the sauce coats the back of a spoon. Strain through a fine-mesh sieve into a bowl. Stir in the vanilla and rum, cover and refrigerate.

To make the pudding, combine the apricots, cherries and liquor in a bowl; let stand for 1 hour. Drain and reserve the fruits and liquor separately.

Preheat an oven to 375°F (190°C). Butter a 2-qt (2-l) baking dish.

In a frying pan over medium-low heat, melt 2 tablespoons of the butter. Add the pears, cover and cook, turning once, until tender, 4–6 minutes. Set aside.

Melt the remaining 4 tablespoons (2 oz/60 g) butter. Place the bread slices on a baking sheet and brush the tops with the melted butter. Place on the top rack of the oven and toast until the edges are golden, about 8 minutes. Remove from the oven and leave the oven set at 375°F (190°C).

Spread one-third of the apricots, cherries, and pears on the bottom of the prepared baking dish. Top with half of the bread, toasted side up, in a single layer. Layer half of the remaining fruits over the bread and top with the remaining bread slices, toasted side up. Scatter on the remaining fruit.

In a saucepan over medium heat, combine the milk, cream, granulated sugar, nutmeg and vanilla. Heat, stirring, until hot, 2–3 minutes; set aside. In a bowl, whisk together the egg yolks, whole eggs and 2 tablespoons reserved liquor. Slowly whisk the milk mixture into the egg mixture. Pour over the bread and fruit.

Put the baking dish in a larger baking pan and add boiling water to the pan to reach halfway up the sides of the dish. Bake until a skewer inserted into the center comes out clean, 50–60 minutes. Let cool for 20 minutes, then dust with confectioners' sugar. Serve with the crème anglaise. *Serves 6*

Let be be finale of seem.
The only emperor is the emperor of ice-cream.

—Wallace Stevens

Wintergreen Ice Cream with Chocolate Truffles

For the ice cream:

2   bunches fresh mint, about 2 oz (60 g) total weight, tough stems removed and leaves coarsely chopped

2   cups (16 fl oz/500 ml) heavy (double) cream

2   cups (16 fl oz/500 ml) milk

⅔ cup (5 oz/155 g) sugar

8   egg yolks

2   tablespoons green crème de menthe

For the chocolate truffles:

5   oz (155 g) bittersweet chocolate, finely chopped

6   tablespoons (3 oz/90 g) unsalted butter, at room temperature

¼   cup (2 fl oz/60 ml) heavy (double) cream

2   teaspoons green crème de menthe

    boiling water, as needed

If you would like to omit the truffles, substitute 6 ounces (185 g) top-quality bittersweet chocolate, coarsely chopped.

TO MAKE THE ICE CREAM, in a saucepan over medium heat, combine the mint, cream, milk and sugar and heat, stirring occasionally, until small bubbles appear along the pan edges. Remove from the heat and let stand for 1 hour.

Meanwhile, make the truffles: Place the chocolate, butter and cream in a heatproof bowl set over a pan of gently simmering water; do not allow the bowl to touch the water. Stir often until the chocolate melts, then immediately remove the bowl from the heat and stir in the crème de menthe. Pour into an 8-inch (20-cm) cake pan and place in the freezer until cold, about 1 hour.

Shape the cold chocolate mixture into truffles: Dip a ½-teaspoon measuring spoon or a tiny melon baller into boiling water, quickly scoop out a truffle and place on a baking sheet. Repeat until all the truffles are formed, arranging them in a single layer and making sure that they do not touch one another. Chill thoroughly in the freezer, about 1 hour.

While the truffles are chilling, finish making the ice cream: Reheat the cream mixture until small bubbles appear along the pan edges. Remove from the heat. In a large bowl, whisk the egg yolks until blended. Slowly pour in the hot cream mixture, whisking constantly. Return the mixture to the saucepan and place over medium heat. Cook, stirring constantly, until the mixture coats the back of a spoon. Strain through a fine-mesh sieve into a clean bowl. Stir in the crème de menthe and refrigerate until cold.

Freeze the ice cream mixture in an ice cream maker according to the manufacturer's instructions. Fold in the chilled truffles during the final 1 minute of freezing. Serve at once or pack into a container and freeze for up to 10 days.
Makes 1½ qt (1.5 l); serves 8

Cranberry Upside-Down Cake

For the topping:

¼   cup (2 oz/60 g) unsalted butter

¾   cup (6 oz/185 g) firmly packed brown sugar

¾   lb (375 g) cranberries

For the cake:

1½   cups (7½ oz/235 g) all-purpose (plain) flour

2   teaspoons baking powder

¼   teaspoon salt

½   cup (4 oz/125 g) unsalted butter

1   cup (8 oz/250 g) granulated sugar

2   eggs, separated

1   teaspoon vanilla extract (essence)

½   cup (4 fl oz/125 ml) milk

⅛   teaspoon cream of tartar

For the whipped cream:

1   cup (8 fl oz/250 ml) heavy (double) cream

¼   teaspoon vanilla extract (essence)

1   tablespoon confectioners' (icing) sugar

This festive holiday cake is inspired by a recipe from Lindsey Shere, pastry chef at Chez Panisse restaurant in Berkeley, California. Fresh cranberries are abundant this time of year, although frozen ones will also work fine.

TO MAKE THE TOPPING, butter a 9-inch (23-cm) round cake pan. Put the butter and brown sugar in the prepared pan and place the pan over medium heat. Heat, stirring occasionally, until the butter is melted and the sugar has dissolved. Scatter the cranberries over the butter–sugar mixture. Set aside.

Preheat an oven to 350°F (180°C).

To make the cake, in a bowl, mix together the flour, baking powder and salt. In another bowl, using an electric mixer set on medium-high speed, beat together the butter and granulated sugar until light and fluffy, 2–3 minutes. Add the egg yolks, one at a time, beating well after each addition. Add the vanilla and mix well. Using a rubber spatula, fold in the flour mixture in 3 batches, adding it alternately with the milk.

In a bowl, using a whisk or an electric mixer, beat the egg whites until soft peaks form. Add the cream of tartar and continue to beat until stiff peaks form. Using the spatula, fold the whites into the batter.

Spoon the batter over the cranberries in the cake pan, spreading it evenly. Bake until a skewer inserted into the center comes out clean, 55–60 minutes. Remove from the oven and let cool on a rack for 15 minutes. Run a knife around the edges of the pan to loosen the cake. Invert onto a serving plate, let stand for 5 minutes, then lift off the pan.

To make the whipped cream, in a bowl, using a whisk or an electric mixer, whip the cream until soft peaks form. Stir in the vanilla and the confectioners' sugar.

To serve, cut the cake into wedges and serve with the whipped cream.

Makes one 9-inch (23-cm) cake; serves 8–10

Citrus Compote with Honey and Golden Raisins

2	cups (16 fl oz/500 ml) sweet dessert wine such as late-harvest Gewürztraminer, late-harvest Riesling, French Sauterne or Muscat de Beaumes-de-Venise
1	cup (8 fl oz/250 ml) fresh orange juice
2	tablespoons honey
½	vanilla bean
½	cup (3 oz/90 g) golden raisins (sultanas)
5	seedless oranges
2	grapefruits *(see note)*
3	kiwifruits

Excellent served on its own, this compote can also be warmed over low heat and spooned over ice cream or sorbet. For the best flavor and most juice, choose pink, red or white grapefruits that are relatively heavy for their size and springy to the touch. The compote can also be made with tangerines, tangelos or blood oranges in place of the oranges and grapefruits.

POUR THE WINE, orange juice and honey into a saucepan. Split the vanilla bean in half lengthwise and, using the tip of a knife, scrape the seeds into the pan. Then add the pod as well and bring to a boil. Reduce the heat to medium and simmer, uncovered, until about 1 cup (8 fl oz/250 ml) remains, about 15 minutes. Remove from the heat and stir in the raisins. Transfer to a bowl and set aside to cool.

Using a sharp knife, cut a thick slice off the top and bottom of each orange to reveal the flesh. Then, standing each orange upright on a cutting surface, cut off the peel and white membrane in thick, wide strips. Working with 1 orange at a time, hold the orange over a bowl and cut along either side of each segment to free it from the membrane, letting the segments drop into the bowl. Repeat this same technique with the grapefruits, using the tip of a knife to remove any seeds.

Peel the kiwifruits. Cut each into 8 wedges and add to the oranges and grapefruits. Add the cooled liquid and raisins, removing the vanilla pod, and stir together.

To serve, spoon the fruit into individual bowls. *Serves 6*

The setting sun, and music at the close,
As the last of sweets, is sweetest last,
Writ in remembrance more than things long past.

—William Shakespeare

Chocolate Hazelnut Torte

For the torte:

½ cup (2½ oz/75 g) hazelnuts (filberts), plus 12 hazelnuts for garnish

6 oz (185 g) bittersweet chocolate, finely chopped

½ cup (4 oz/125 g) unsalted butter, at room temperature

⅔ cup (5 oz/155 g) plus 2 tablespoons sugar

5 eggs, separated

¼ cup (1½ oz/45 g) all-purpose (plain) flour

¼ cup (¾ oz/20 g) unsweetened cocoa

⅛ teaspoon cream of tartar

For the glaze:

9 oz (280 g) bittersweet chocolate, finely chopped

¾ cup (6 oz/185 g) unsalted butter, at room temperature, cut into small pieces

1½ tablespoons light corn syrup

PREHEAT AN OVEN to 375°F (190°C). Lightly butter and flour a 9-inch (23-cm) round springform cake pan.

To make the torte, spread the ½ cup (2½ oz/75 g) nuts on a baking sheet and toast in the oven until lightly browned and fragrant, 5–7 minutes. While the nuts are still warm, place them in a kitchen towel and rub with the towel to remove the skins. Do not worry if bits of skin remain. Set aside.

Place the chocolate and butter in a large heatproof bowl set over (not touching) gently simmering water in a pan. Stir often until the chocolate melts, then remove from the heat.

In a food processor fitted with the metal blade or in a blender, combine the skinned nuts with the ⅔ cup (5 oz/155 g) sugar. Pulse until finely ground. Add to the chocolate mixture and stir until blended. Let cool; then, one at a time, add the egg yolks, beating well after each addition. In a bowl, sift together the flour and cocoa. Stir into the chocolate mixture.

In another bowl, using an electric mixer, beat the egg whites and cream of tartar until soft peaks form. Add the 2 tablespoons sugar and beat until stiff peaks form. Using a rubber spatula, fold one-fourth of the whites into the chocolate mixture to lighten it. Fold in the remaining whites just until no white streaks remain. Pour into the prepared pan.

Bake until a skewer inserted into the center comes out almost clean, 35–40 minutes. Let cool in the pan on a rack.

To make the glaze, combine the chocolate, butter and corn syrup in a heatproof bowl set over (not touching) gently simmering water in a pan. Stir often until the chocolate melts, then remove from the heat. Stir until smooth. Let cool, stirring occasionally, for 15 minutes; it will thicken slightly.

Invert the torte onto the rack set over a baking sheet and lift off the pan. Pour on the glaze, tilting the torte to coat the top and sides completely. When the glaze stops dripping, place the 12 hazelnuts around the top of the cake. Transfer to a serving plate and serve. *Makes one 9-inch (23-cm) torte; serves 10*

Love and eggs are best when they are fresh.

—Russian Proverb

Grand Marnier Soufflé

For the soufflé dish:

18 ladyfingers

3 tablespoons Grand Marnier

For the soufflé batter:

4 egg yolks

½ cup (4 oz/120 g) sugar

3 tablespoons unsalted butter

3 tablespoons all-purpose (plain) flour

pinch of salt

1 cup (8 fl oz/250 ml) milk

5 egg whites

¼ teaspoon cream of tartar

2 tablespoons Grand Marnier

1 teaspoon finely grated orange zest

Since wintertime entertaining is often elegant, this featherlight soufflé is a favorite of the season. Have your guests seated at the table so that you can serve the soufflé the moment it is taken from the oven.

PREHEAT AN OVEN to 375°F (190°C). Butter a 1½-qt (1.5-l) soufflé dish or six 1-cup (8-fl oz/250-ml) ramekins and dust with sugar. Place the ladyfingers on a work surface and sprinkle the Grand Marnier evenly over them; if using ramekins, cut the ladyfingers in half crosswise. Line the sides of the dish(es) with the ladyfingers, standing them upright and close together.

To make the soufflé batter, in a bowl, using an electric mixer set on medium-high speed, beat together the egg yolks and ¼ cup (2 oz/60 g) of the sugar until light colored, about 1 minute. In a small saucepan over low heat, melt the butter. Add the flour and salt and whisk for 1 minute. Gradually stir in the milk and cook, stirring, until the mixture is smooth and thick, 3–4 minutes. Remove from the heat and gradually whisk the milk mixture into the yolk-sugar mixture. Return the mixture to the saucepan and place over medium heat. Continue to cook, stirring, until the mixture coats the back of a spoon, about 1 minute. Remove from the heat and let cool.

Place the egg whites in a heatproof bowl. Place the bowl over a pan of hot water to warm the whites slightly; do not allow the bowl to touch the water. Remove the bowl from the heat and add the cream of tartar. Using a clean whisk or an electric mixer, beat the whites until soft peaks form. Add the remaining ¼ cup (2 oz/60 g) sugar and beat until stiff peaks form.

Using a rubber spatula, fold about one-fourth of the whites into the cooled sauce to lighten it. Fold in the remaining whites just until no white streaks remain. Stir in the Grand Marnier and orange zest.

Pour the batter into the prepared dish(es). Bake until set but the center still jiggles slightly when the dish is gently shaken, about 40 minutes for the large soufflé or 15–20 minutes for the small ones. Serve at once. *Serves 6*

acknowledgments

The following kindly lent props for photography: The Gardener, Berkeley, CA; Fillamento, San Francisco, CA;
American Rag, San Francisco, CA; Table Prop, San Francisco, CA; Missy Pepper; Chuck Williams; Williams-Sonoma and Pottery Barn.
The publishers would also like to thank Sarah Lemas and Ken DellaPenta for their editorial assistance.
Thanks also goes to Penina and Michelle Syracuse for surfaces used in photography, and to Lisa Atwood,
Joanne Leese, Kathy Myers, Jean Tenanes and Paul Weir for their support to the author.